Courage for the Earth

Courage *for the* Earth

Writers, Scientists, and Activists Celebrate the Life and Writing of RACHEL CARSON

Edited by Peter Matthiessen

A MARINER ORIGINAL
HOUGHTON MIFFLIN COMPANY
Boston · New York 2007

Visit our Web site: www.houghtonmifflinbooks.com.

Library of Congress Cataloging-in-Publication Data

Courage for the Earth : writers, scientists, and activists celebrate the life and writing of Rachel Carson / edited by Peter Matthiessen.
p. cm.
Includes bibliographical references.
ISBN-13: 978-0-618-87276-3
ISBN-10: 0-618-87276-0
1. Carson, Rachel, 1907–1964. Silent spring. 2. Pesticides—Environmental aspects. 3. Carson, Rachel, 1907–1964.
I. Matthiessen, Peter.
QH545.P4C684 2007 577.27'9—dc22 2006103363

Printed in the United States of America

Book design by Robert Overholtzer

MP 10 9 8 7 6 5 4 3 2 1

Contents

5/07

Courage for the Earth

PETER MATTHIESSEN

Introduction

SHE WAS ALWAYS a writer and she always knew that. Like Faulkner, Fitzgerald, Edna St. Vincent Millay, and other American contemporaries with the same affliction, ten-year-old Rachel Louise Carson, born in 1907 in the Allegheny Valley in Springdale, Pennsylvania, was first published in the *St. Nicholas* literary magazine for children. A loner and a reader and a devotee of birds and indeed all nature, the slim, shy girl of plain face and dark curly hair continued writing throughout adolescence: she chose an English major at Pennsylvania College for Women and continued to submit poetry to periodicals. Not until her junior year, when a biology course reawakened the "sense of wonder" with which she had always encountered the natural world, did she switch her major to zoology, still unaware that these passions might be complementary.

Graduating magna cum laude in 1929, Carson went on

to Johns Hopkins to complete her master's degree in zoology, but increasing family responsibilities caused her to abandon her quest for a doctorate. For a few years she would teach zoology at the University of Maryland, continuing her studies in the summer at the Marine Biological Laboratory in Woods Hole, Massachusetts. It was there, in her early twenties, that she first fell under the spell of the eternal mysteries of the sea.

In 1932, "Ray" Carson, as some friends knew her, took part-time work as a writer-editor for the old Bureau of Fisheries, a job that led, in 1936, to a full-time appointment as a junior aquatic biologist. To eke out her small salary, she contributed feature articles to the *Baltimore Sun*, most of them related to marine fisheries and the sea. Though her poetry was never to be published, a strong lyrical prose was already evolving, and one of her pieces for a government publication seemed to the editor so elegant and unusual that he urged her to submit it to the *Atlantic Monthly*.

> Thus . . . the parts of the plan fall into place: the water receiving from earth and air the simple materials, storing them until the gathering energy of the spring sun wakens the sleeping plants to a burst of dynamic activity, hungry swarms of planktonic animals growing and multiplying upon the abundant plants, and themselves falling prey to the shoals of fish; all, in the end, to be redissolved into their component substances . . . Individual elements are lost to view, only to reappear again and again in different incarnations in a kind of material immortality.

"Undersea," the young writer's first publication in a national magazine (September 1937), was seminal in theme and tone to all her later writing. Together with an evocative *Sun* feature, "Chesapeake Eels Seek the Sargasso Sea" ("From every river and stream along the whole Atlantic Coast, eels are hurrying to the sea . . ."), it was the starting point for her first book, *Under the Sea-Wind.* Though its feeling was near-mystical — the ever-changing changelessness of life on earth — the book's method took after *Salar the Salmon* and *Taka the Otter*, two popular tales by the British writer Henry Williamson. (Carson's other revered Henrys were Thoreau, Beston (*The Outermost House*), and Tomlinson, the literary editor of the *Nation and Athenaeum*, whose vacation chronicle, *The Sea and the Jungle*, described a voyage from England to South America, then up the Amazon; *The Sea and the Jungle* may well be the finest writing on the sea, Conrad included.) Like Williamson, Carson used anthropomorphic characters to carry the narrative, notably Scomber the Mackerel (from *Scomber scombrus*, the Atlantic mackerel's taxonomic name).

> He came into being as a tiny globule no larger than a poppy seed, drifting in the surface layers of pale-green water. The globule carried an amber droplet of oil that served to keep it afloat and it carried also a gray particle of living matter so small that it could have been picked up on the point of a needle. In time this particle was to become Scomber, the mackerel, a powerful fish, streamlined after the manner of his kind, and a rover of the seas.

However, the real protagonist of this work (as of its better known successors) was the sea itself — "whether I wished it or not," as Carson explained in her original foreword, "for the sense of the sea, holding the power of life and death over every one of its creatures from the smallest to the largest, would inevitably pervade every page."

> To stand at the edge of the sea, to sense the ebb and flow of the tides, to feel the breath of a mist moving over a great salt marsh, to watch the flight of shorebirds that have swept up and down the surf lines of the continents for untold thousands of years, to see the running of the old eels and the young shad to the sea, is to have knowledge of things that are as nearly eternal as any earthly life can be. These things were before man ever stood on the shore of the ocean and looked out upon it with wonder; they continue year in, year out, throughout the centuries and ages, while man's kingdoms rise and fall.

Under the Sea-Wind was to remain Carson's favorite among her books. Published in 1941, on the eve of World War II, it sold less than two thousand copies and passed almost unnoticed. Meanwhile, the Bureau of Fisheries had joined in 1940 with the old Biological Survey to become the Fish and Wildlife Service, and her editorial duties had increased, together with her biological assignments; she was specializing now in marine zoology and was later promoted to chief editor of publications.

Although gentle with contributors, Carson the editor (according to her colleagues) could be "tart and wry" about lackluster writing. Toward her own work, she was ever more rigorous and demanding, not only in regard to the depth and breadth of her research but in the economy and clarity of her style, which she revised, read aloud, and tightened with the glad exhilaration of the born writer.

Colleagues enjoyed working with her because of her uncommon competence and dedication but also because of her childlike enthusiasm and undiminished wonder at the myriad ways of nature, which made a scientific expedition out of the simplest foray into field or tide pool. In their first meeting, the naturalist Louis Halle *(Springtime in Washington)* found Carson "quiet, diffident, neat, proper, and without affectation — serious, dignified, with a gentle voice." Nothing written about her since seems to dispute this. But for all her modesty and restraint, she had confidence in her own literary worth and was neither prim nor meek; she had a mischievous streak and an edge to her tongue, and once she was published, became an astute businesswoman and career tactician.

A decade after Carson's first book, her agent, Marie Rodell, circulated a second work in progress that proposed to explore the origins and geological aspects of the sea. Already the author was corresponding with marine scientists everywhere and had even embarked on a Woods Hole research vessel for a sea voyage — her first and last — to the Georges Banks. Because her first book was unsuccessful and its author little known, the new one was widely rejected, despite strong endorsements and support from such influential eminences as the great Woods Hole oceanographer Dr. Henry Bigelow, Dr. Robert C. Murphy of the

American Museum of Natural History, Dr. William Beebe of the New York Zoological Society, Thor Heyerdahl of Kon-tiki, and the best-selling naturalist-writer Edwin Way Teale. The material was refused by fifteen magazines, including *National Geographic.* In September 1950, however, a section titled "The Birth of an Island" appeared in the *Yale Review;* another section was subsequently accepted by *Science Digest.* Eventually the material came into the hands of Edith Oliver at *The New Yorker,* who recommended it to William Shawn, who recognized its exceptional quality at once. Much of it was serialized as "A Profile of the Sea," and in July of the following year, the whole manuscript was published as *The Sea Around Us.* It won the John Burroughs Medal, then the National Book Award, and within the year sold more than 200,000 copies in hardcover. (*Under the Sea-Wind*, resurrected, was to join it for a prolonged stay on the bestseller list.)

What came across in all of Carson's work was what Alfred Schweitzer called "a reverence for life." Accused of "ignoring God" in *The Sea Around Us*, she responded, "As far as I am concerned, there is absolutely no conflict between a belief in evolution and a belief in God as the creator. Believing as I do in evolution, I merely believe that is the method by which God created, and is still creating, life on earth. And it is a method so marvelously conceived that to study it in detail is to increase — and certainly never to diminish — one's reverence and awe both for the Creator and the process."

Although the sea was her obsession, Carson wrote beautifully on other subjects, from the threat of nuclear technology and the first signs of global warming to animal rights and the importance of introducing nature to young children. She was always interested in the writing process, understanding that "the writer must never try to impose himself upon his subject. He must not try to mold it according to what he believes his readers or editors want to read. His initial task is to come to know his subject intimately, to understand its every aspect, to let it fill his mind. Then at some turning point the subject takes command and the true act of creation begins." In combining her writing with a career in science, she had what she once called "the magic combination of factual knowledge and deeply felt emotional response."

In accepting the National Book Award in 1952, with cowinners James Jones and Marianne Moore, she said, "There is no such thing as a separate literature of science, since the aim of science is to discover and illuminate the truth, which is also the aim of all true literature." As Paul Brooks, her friend and editor at Houghton Mifflin, comments in *Rachel Carson: The Writer at Work*, "As a writer she used words to reveal the poetry — which is to say the essential truth and meaning — at the core of any scientific fact. She sought the knowledge that is essential to appreciate the extent of the unknown."

Success permitted Carson to retire from the FWS in 1952 and write full-time. The following summer she bought land and built a cottage on the Sheepscot River near West

Southport on the coast of Maine, where she and her mother had visited since 1946. Maria Carson, a kindred spirit in her nature study, had been subtly possessive of her gentle daughter, whom she encouraged to support several family members in addition to herself. Her mother, who died in 1958, is generally accounted responsible for the fact that Carson never married and had children, although she would adopt her sister's orphaned son. In an article of this period called "Help Your Child to Wonder," Carson expressed her intense belief in the importance of nature study for the young.

> A child's world is fresh and new and beautiful, full of wonder and excitement. It is our misfortune that for most of us that clear-eyed vision, that true instinct for what is beautiful and awe-inspiring, is dimmed and even lost before we reach adulthood . . . The years of early childhood are the time to prepare the soil. Once the emotions have been aroused — a sense of the beautiful, the excitement of the new and the unknown, a feeling of sympathy, pity, admiration or love — then we wish for knowledge . . . Once found, it has lasting meaning. It is more important to pave the way for the child to want to know than to put him on a diet of facts he is not ready to assimilate.

During her Maine summers Carson was active in local conservation efforts and engaged, as she did everywhere, in the close examination of nature, from rocks to insects to marine flora. Nothing was lost on her.

> [The firefly] was flying so low over the water that his light cast a long surface reflection, like a little headlight. Then

> the truth dawned on me. He "thought" the flashes in the water [the phosphorescence of sparkling diatoms thrown up by small breaking waves] were other fireflies, signalling to him in the age-old manner of fireflies. Sure enough, he was soon in trouble and we saw his light flashing urgently as he was rolled around in the wet sand. (*From a letter to Dorothy and Stanley Freeman, 1956*)

By now, *The New Yorker* had serialized *The Edge of the Sea*, the third volume of her marine trilogy, which evoked the ecology of maritime communities on three types of coast — the rock-bound shores north of Cape Cod, ruled by the tides; the sand beaches to the south of it, ruled by the waves; and the coral reefs of southern Florida, whose ecology is mainly determined by the ocean currents. This book, which was also a bestseller, was followed in March of the following year by a Carson-scripted television film on clouds called *Something About the Sky*.

Carson's new celebrity had given her the confidence and opportunity to speak out strongly for the environmental cause. In an op-ed letter to the *Washington Post* condemning the ouster by the new Republican administration of a competent and principled secretary of the interior, Albert M. Day, in favor of the crass, partisan political appointee Benton McKay, she found the cool and furious tone that would serve her well in *Silent Spring* a few years later.

> For many years public-spirited citizens throughout the country have been working for the conservation of natural resources, realizing their vital importance to the Nation.

> Apparently their hard-won progress is to be wiped out, as a politically-minded Administration returns us to the dark ages of unrestrained exploitation and destruction. It is one of the ironies of our time that, while concentrating on the defense of our country against enemies from without, we should be so heedless of those who would destroy it from within.

She could have signed that identical letter today.

As early as 1945, Carson and her close colleague Dr. Clarence Cottam had become alarmed by government abuse of new chemical insecticides such as DDT. Most of these highly toxic materials had been derived from lethal compounds developed originally for use in war; the "predator" and "pest" control programs, in particular, which were broadcasting poisons with little regard for the welfare of other creatures. That same year, she offered an article to *Reader's Digest* on insecticide experiments going on in nearby Patuxent, Maryland, not far from her home in Silver Spring, to determine the effects of DDT on valuable insects as well as on birds and other life. The *Digest* was not interested, though *Harper's* and the *Atlantic Monthly* had published articles by others that same year that warned of the dangers of DDT to the balance of nature. Carson went back to her government job and her sea trilogy, and not until after the third volume had been completed did she return to this earlier preoccupation.

By that time, the insecticide barrage had been augmented by dieldrin, parathion, heptachlor, malathion, and other fearful compounds many times stronger than DDT, all of which the government planned to distribute through the Department of Agriculture for public use and commercial manufacture. "The more I learned about the use of pesticides, the more appalled I became," Carson recalled. "I realized that here was the material for a book. What I discovered was that everything which meant most to me as a naturalist was being threatened, and that nothing I could do would be more important." She intended to make certain that if the public continued to let itself be led by politicians who stood by and permitted the looting of world resources and the pollution of the land, air, and water that our children must inherit, it would not be because we knew no better.

With her fame, eloquence, and reputation for precision, Carson could count on the support of the leading scientists and conservation organizations and was well positioned to command a hearing. Even so, the *Digest* and other magazines had little interest in her gloomy subject. Then, in 1957, came a startling wildlife mortality in the wake of a mosquito control campaign near Duxbury, Massachusetts, followed by a pointless spraying of a DDT/fuel-oil mix over eastern Long Island for eradication of the gypsy moth. Next, an all-out war in the Southern states against the fire ant did such widespread damage that its own beneficiaries cried out for mercy, and after that a great furor arose over the spraying of cranberry plants with aminotriazol, which led to a Department of Agriculture ban against all cranberry marketing, just in time for Thanksgiving 1959.

"During the past 15 years," Carson protested in a letter

that year to the *Washington Post*, "the use of highly poisonous hydrocarbons and organophosphates allied to the nerve gases of chemical warfare built up from small beginnings to what a noted British ecologist recently called 'an amazing rain of death upon the surface of the earth.' Most of these chemicals have long-persisting residues on vegetation, in soils, and even in the bodies of earthworms and other organisms . . . If this 'rain of death' has produced such a disastrous effect on birds, what of other lives, including our own?"

Earlier that year, the ornithologist Roger Tory Peterson, alarmed by the falloff in bird numbers, had declared that the current broadcasting of lethal chemicals was the greatest threat to wildlife of all time. DDT had been classified as a "chemical carcinogen" by one of Carson's informants, Dr. Wilhelm Hueper of the National Cancer Institute (who found Carson "a sincere, unusually well-informed scientist possessing not only an unusual degree of social responsibility but also having the courage and ability to express and fight for her convictions and principles"). She was fighting more desperately than he knew. In 1960, Rachel Carson had learned that her doctors had misdiagnosed what turned out to be a fatal breast cancer. Despite a mastectomy and debilitating illness, she would persevere in the most demanding book she had ever written.

As a new writer in this period, I was reading all her books with the greatest admiration as fast as they appeared. By ill luck, I never met Carson, although I worked with some of her FWS colleagues, including Dr. Clarence Cottam and also Bob Hines, whose superb line drawings illustrated *The Edge of the Sea* and also *Wildlife in America*, my own contribution to the new environmental movement. Though that book and others had already denounced the indiscriminate broadcasting of pesticides by the time *Silent Spring* appeared, it was Carson who hit upon the brilliant metaphor that drew all these warnings to a point:

> There was once a town in the heart of America where all life seemed to live in harmony with its surroundings . . . Then a strange blight crept over the area and everything began to change . . . There was a strange stillness . . . The few birds seen anywhere were moribund: they trembled violently and could not fly. It was a spring without voices. On the mornings that had once throbbed with the dawn chorus . . . of scores of bird voices there was now no sound; only silence lay over the fields and woods and marsh.

That same year, E. B. White had recommended Carson's project to William Shawn at *The New Yorker*. In January 1960, delighted by Shawn's response to her material, she wrote to her friend Dorothy Freeman, "Suddenly the tension of four years was broken and I let the tears come. I think I let you see last summer what my deeper feelings are . . . when I said I could never again listen happily to a thrush song if I had not done all I could. And last night the thoughts of all the birds and other creatures and all the loveliness that is in nature came to me with such a surge of deep happiness that now I had done what I could — I had been able to complete it — now it had its own life."

Silent Spring, serialized in *The New Yorker* in June and July 1962, gored corporate oxen all over the country. Even before publication, Carson was violently assailed by lawsuits and derision, including suggestions that this meticulous scientist (whose master's thesis had been titled "The Development of the Pronephros During the Embryonic and Early Larval Life of the Catfish (*Ictalurus punctatus*)" was a "hysterical woman" unqualified to write such a subversive book. For *Silent Spring* had dared to say, among many other unconscionable things, "This is an era dominated by industry, in which the right to make a dollar at whatever cost is seldom challenged." A huge counterattack was organized and led by Monsanto, Velsicol, American Cyanamid — indeed, the whole chemical industry, duly supported by the Department of Agriculture as well as the domesticated ostriches in the media. (*Time*'s reviewer deplored Carson's "over-simplifications and downright errors . . . Many of the scary generalizations — and there are lots of them — are patently unsound.") *Reader's Digest* tagged along with an abridgment of the *Time* review, with which it replaced its own canceled condensation of the original. (Seven years later, in April 1969, *Time* would feel obliged to run Carson's photo at the head of an environmental article citing new evidence that completely supported the data in *Silent Spring*.)

By year's end, *Audubon* and *National Parks* magazine had published additional excerpts from the book, and all but the most self-serving of Carson's attackers were backing rapidly toward safer ground. In their ugly campaign to reduce a brave scientist's protest to a matter of public relations, the chemical interests had only increased public awareness. *Silent Spring* became a runaway bestseller, with international reverberations. In the next two years, in what the author herself called "an extraordinary constellation of events," Carson was awarded the Audubon Medal and numerous honors, including election to the American Academy of Arts and Letters, in homage to her rare literary gifts. Nearly fifty years later, the book is still regarded as the cornerstone of the new environmentalism movement. Well crafted, fearless, and succinct, it remains her most celebrated book, although her wonderful essays on the world around us may be remembered longer.

Though she worked in nonfiction, Rachel Carson understood the task of all good writing as a work of creation: "The writer moves into a realm where he had never been before — perhaps where no one has ever been. It is a lonely place, and even a little frightening." Famed as a scientist whose timely book on chemical poisons had served as a warning to the world about the insatiable nature of corporate greed, she was at the same time an important writer, one of the finest nature writers of her century. And it is for her literary excellence, not her cry of warning, that in the end, she may be best remembered.

Off the shore from her Maine cottage is an island forested in spruce, which Carson invested with many lovely reveries.

> The island voice which came . . . most beautifully and clearly each evening was the voice of a forest spirit, the hermit thrush. At the hour of the evening's beginning its broken and silvery cadences drifted with infinite deliberation across the water. Its phrases were filled with a beauty and a meaning that were not wholly of the present, as though the thrush were singing of other sunsets, extending far back beyond his personal memory, through eons of time when his forebears had known this place, and from spruce trees long since returned to earth had sung the beauty of the evening.

Perhaps the imminence of her own mortality had helped her find her precious balance and perspective. In most photographs, the pensive face appears a little sad, but this was true long before she knew that she had cancer. And surely a lingering sadness is unavoidable for all who revere the natural world and bear witness to its ongoing degradation, as the rightful heritage of our children and grandchildren diminishes day by day. "Of course I felt special sympathy with your thoughts on 'the secret tension between love [of nature] and despair' so that 'no carefree love of the planet is now possible.' Each day those words become more true!" she wrote to her friend Lois Crisler, author of *Arctic Wild.* Carson died at the age of fifty-six, in April 1964, in Maryland.

> Sometimes I would watch the island from the hill that sloped up from the water line . . . The woods . . . were bright with the moving, flitting forms of many warblers — the exquisite powder-blue parula with his breast band

> of orange and magenta; the Blackburnian, like flickering flames in the spruces; the myrtle, flashing his yellow rump patch. But most numerous of all was the trim little black-throated green warbler, whose dreamy, nostalgic song drifted all day long through the woods, little wisps of song lingering like bits of fog in the tree tops. (*unpublished essay*)

"The beauty of the living world I was trying to save," she wrote in a letter to a friend in 1962, "has always been uppermost in my mind — that, and anger at the senseless, brutish things that were being done. I have felt bound by a solemn obligation to do what I could — if I didn't at least try I could never be happy again in nature. But now I can believe that I have at least helped a little. It would be unrealistic to believe one book could bring a complete change."

Sadly, the damage to wildlife being done by poison chemicals today is far worse than it was when she wrote her book. When *Silent Spring* was published, I could still count sixteen species of wood warblers in May migration on my own small property on the northeast Atlantic coast, and several species of shy woodland thrushes appeared regularly in spring and fall. In recent years, I have seen fewer than sixteen warblers of *all* species during spring migration, and a few hermit thrushes only. While this "silent spring" is not entirely attributable to pesticides, one shudders to imagine nonetheless how much more impoverished our habitat would be had Rachel Carson not sounded the alarm.

Rachel Carson was not a born crusader but an intelligent and dedicated woman who rose heroically to the occasion. Rightly confident about her facts as well as her ability to present them, secure in the approval of her peers, she remained serene in the face of her accusers. Throughout her life, she was brave and fierce in defense of what she held most sacred, which was the wonder of life and all its creatures, even such malignant creatures as ourselves.

EDITOR'S NOTE: The "courage" in the title of this fine variegated collection is rightly celebrated in virtually every essay in this book, including my own introduction, and this dedicated bravery of Rachel Carson, born of a quiet self-assurance, can scarcely be overpraised. Her tenacity withstood the subversion, slander, and mendacity of our greedy industries and corporations and their errand boys in Congress and the media—forces that for long decades, doing great harm to their own country and the citizen-consumers who have made them so wealthy, have defeated any lasting progress against the pollution of our environment by chemical wastes and inefficient, filthy, and toxic fossil fuels.

As a dying woman all too aware that her time was running out even as she struggled to finish *Silent Spring*, Rachel Carson also left us prescient warnings — largely subverted or ignored — about the sickening of oceans and the contamination of the earth's climate, already manifesting the first symptoms of what all but hired scientists have come to recognize as global warming.

Again, I agree with more than one of the excellent essayists in this volume that in years to come, a time-bound tract such as *Silent Spring*, for all its eloquence and deserved renown, may not be esteemed quite so highly as the beautiful writings and responses that record Rachel Carson's thoughts and observations in the field of the life of seas and songbirds. In her lyrical intuitions and extraordinary ear for the precision and balance of well-fashioned English sentences, her work transcends most so-called nature writing, earning a place as real literature beyond all genres that will endure to inspire those who follow. Rachel Carson is still insufficiently recognized for what she is and always will be, an American writer who escapes her several categories to endow us with some of the finest prose in the English language. — P.M.

LINDA LEAR

Love, Fear, and Witnessing

WHEN I WROTE *Rachel Carson: Witness for Nature* in 1997, my hope was to dismiss for all time the notion of Carson as an iconic goddess who fearlessly battled the giants of science and industry for the rights of nature. I wanted to replace this stubborn idea with a real woman, one whose life and work were shaped by the collapse of certainty and the possibility of annihilation.

Carson certainly was fearless. Her courage helped change the way we now look at the natural world. But she was also deeply driven, and often emotionally remote to others. She was a woman who knew in her inner core that she had an "obligation to endure" and that there was work for her to do; but the doing was as full of pain and pathos as it was of wonder and warning. I hoped to make clear these fully human aspects of Carson's life and thereby to open it to examination and elaboration. Carson was aware from a young age that she had been given a very special gift of language, and like the opera diva, conscious of the power of her beautiful voice, she used it to defend what she loved.

As a biologist and a naturalist, Carson had a rare gift of observation and the spiritual quality of wonder and awe that enabled her to extend her curiosity about meaning to a microcosm in ways few of us have time or patience to consider. Her love of the natural world allowed no separation between observed fact and the ethical responsibility to make that understanding part of public dialogue. Advocacy was inseparable from knowledge and understanding. Describing life as a biologist and compelling us to action as a polemicist was not intellectually debatable. It was an inherent moral obligation for those who loved the natural world. Although it brought her criticism, abuse, and dismissal, she had no real choice. Her understanding of the existential meaning of a thing was always translated by her prose into the "real world." Whether it was her concern for teaching biological ethics in the high school laboratory, or her writing about cruelty to animals raised for slaughter, or her reverence for the smallest life forms, her concerns were part and parcel of what she perceived of the ebb and flow of life. That same concern for the holistic relationship between living things led her to investigate the misuse of chemical pesticides and the potential death of nature. In each instance, Rachel Carson was, through her literary genius, able to translate her love and her fear in such measure that the citizen/reader could accept her message as a testament of integrity, untainted either by ego or agenda.

Carson's witness for nature was a witness against destruction. Her enemy was human arrogance that abrogated the rights of nonhuman nature and assumed eternal regeneration of the environment regardless of assault. Her critique of such hubris — whether in the academy, in the laboratory, in industry, on the farm, or in the home — animates all her writing. Carson's alarm may well have had its birth in her Calvinist upbringing, but if it did, it was reinforced by her early life near Pittsburgh, Pennsylvania, a city contaminated through industrial arrogance and disrespect, and by her experience of the environmental impact of such carelessness.

Carson was an evolutionist who found no inconsistency in celebrating a divine design. She was a spiritualist who needed no theological creed when there was the promise of "material immortality" in the endless recycling of all life in the sea. Ultimately her protest was against existential meaninglessness, against the culture of destruction and annihilation. Her best writing broadened the definitions of human responsibility and relationship and provided comfort and hope.

Reflecting on Carson's life in the years since I finished my biography, I have come to think that her witness for the unity of life, and the holism of her ethic as expressed in her trilogy on the sea, may ultimately be more important than her exposure of the dangers of pesticide contamination for the future of humans and the natural world. Understandably this body of work has taken second place to the controversy over pesticide use. It is time for a reexamination of

Carson's pioneering work in ocean ecology and, ultimately, for a reconsideration of her environmental ethics.

Silent Spring was unabashedly a work of both science and literature. No one was more keenly aware of this than Carson herself. It was a subject she tried to avoid writing about. There was so much else she wanted to say if only she had time enough: the necessity of wonder, the meaning of ecology. Her sea books were about life and renewal prompted by love of the mysterious and the awe-full, whereas *Silent Spring* was, as her editor Paul Brooks once remarked, a book about death, prompted by anger.

Her view of nature and ultimately of life was, I believe, ocean-centered. Her field notes from her memorable trip aboard a research vessel sent from Woods Hole Marine Biological Laboratory in Massachusetts to the Georges Bank in 1948 tell of her profound connection to the undersea world, to the secret life of microorganisms, and to her desire to decipher the movement of tides and the development of islands. But her very first essay, "Undersea," was also a work that followed flows: flows of rivers to oceans, of oceans back to estuaries, of the recycling of life, and of seabirds and fish that respond to ancient signals that struck her full of wonder. The essay reflects only the most fleeting encounter with human life, and that, I believe, was inserted by editorial directive. Oceana's mysteriousness drew Carson first into literature and later into biology. Her preferred universe was one of water. The wonders of the deep dominated her curiosity, and the recycling of life gave ontological meaning to the panorama of life that she discovered in a tide pool. The tide pool came to stand as the encapsulation of all life, and she used it with memorable metaphorical skill in *The Edge of the Sea.* In real life, her greatest joy was to go down to the tide pools at night, flashlight in hand, to listen to sounds of the water, and to return to the sea the creature or the plant that had captured her fascination.

The ocean had a voice to which Carson could give literary expression as well as scientific identification. She had been intrigued by William Beebe's research in sonar recordings of life in the deep-ocean floor. Shy and lacking confidence as a public speaker, Carson hid behind the recorded sounds of shrimp mating in her first public lecture after the publication of *The Sea Around Us.* She was profoundly moved by Beebe's recordings of sounds made by the catch brought up on ship's deck and then lowered back to the ocean. Roaming the marginal coastal beaches of the Carolinas, she expanded her philosophical understanding of life and death by observing the migration of eels. Her oceanographic mentors were Hendrick van Loon, Thor Heyerdahl, and Otto Pettersson, whose sea adventures always included the voices of birds as well as the iridescent signals of bottom dwellers. Sound, sight, air, and water: these are the elements on which Carson's craft was based and which she painted indelibly in words.

Although Carson's mother was a pianist, Carson came late to an appreciation of symphonic music. She wrote the jacket notes for a new RCA Victor recording of Claude Debussy's *La Mer* in 1951, but her comments are more reflective of how such music strengthened the spirit in times of tribulation and allowed a contemplation of beauty and mystery, and less specific on the composition itself. It was her friend Dorothy Freeman who awakened in Carson the capacity to listen fully to music. Perhaps the musical expression of beauty was too intimate and too overwhelming for a woman who kept tight control of her emotions. But their shared appreciation of Beethoven's great violin concerto brought comfort to Carson as nothing else when at last she had finished *Silent Spring* and had the satisfaction of knowing that her creation "was good."

Carson was solitary because she understood herself first and foremost as a writer. She was, as all good writers are, obsessed with her work, with the glimpse of perfection, and with the pleasure writing gave her. As a woman in the 1950s, marriage and motherhood would only have diluted her energy and compromised her mission. Cancer was an intervention in that witness. She held her illness at bay both by courageous denial on the one hand and by fearless participation in her own medical treatment on the other. There were compelling reasons for her silence about her struggle against her cancer, personal and political, but because of her silence we are deprived of her witness to dying.

If time had been left to her, some of it would have been given to animal welfare, to the cultivation of wonder, the conservation of native plants, especially wildflowers, the preservation of seashores, and to the philosophy of ecology. She was passionate about the growing contamination of the oceans. Her last public address warned of its coming and of its certain repercussions. It is my hope that those who read the writing in this book will be moved to carry forward Rachel Carson's love of the stream of life. As contemporary society moves ever closer to the abyss, it is well to remember her vision as much as her alarm.

EDWARD O. WILSON

On *Silent Spring*

FORTY YEARS AGO, *Silent Spring* delivered a galvanic jolt to public consciousness and, as a result, infused the environmental movement with new substance and meaning. The effects of pesticides and other toxic chemical pollutants on the environment and public health had been well documented before *Silent Spring*, but in bits and pieces scattered through the technical literature. Environmental scientists were aware of the problem, but by and large they focused only on the narrow sector of their personal expertise. It was Rachel Carson's achievement to synthesize this knowledge into a single image that everyone, scientists and the general public alike, could easily understand.

The need for such a book was great even within the sciences. As the mild-mannered aquatic biologist was researching *Silent Spring*, ecology was near the bottom of the scientific disciplines in prestige and support; few Americans even knew what the word meant. Conservation biology, later to become one of the most rapidly growing disciplines, did not exist. At the time, the scientific culture was fixated on the spectacular success of the molecular revolution, which had placed physics and chemistry at the foundation of biology. Researchers were learning to reduce living processes to their molecular elements. I, for example, as a young naturalist trained in field biology, was busy collaborating with organic chemists to break the code of pheromones used by ants to organize their colonies.

The environment was also excluded from the mainstream political agenda. America in the late 1950s and early 1960s was an exuberant and prospering nation. Buoyed by record peacetime economic growth, an ethic of limitless progress prevailed, yet the country, locked in a cold war that threatened our way of life, was vulnerable to the formidable enemies that encircled us. The Soviet Union had matched the United States in nuclear weaponry and beaten us into space, and on the Asian mainland China held us at a military standstill. For the sake of our prosperity and security, we rewarded science and technology with high esteem and placed great trust in the seeming infallibility of material ingenuity. As a consequence, environmental warnings were treated with irritable impatience. To a populace whose forebears had within living memory colonized the interior of a vast continent and whose country had never lost a war, arguments for limit and constraint seemed almost unpatriotic.

The temper of the times was epitomized by the concept of the peaceful use of atoms, which culminated in federal plans to excavate harbors and waterways with low-yield nuclear explosions. One such proposal seriously considered by engineers was the instant construction of a sea-level channel parallel to the Panama Canal with a string of precisely timed detonations. Fortunately, that particular dream never left the drawing board. Aside from the foreign policy complications inherent in cutting a Central American country into two pieces, there was a biological risk. The U.S. National Research Council committee reviewing the plan (on which I served as a junior member) raised a warning hand. We pointed out that organisms living in the shallow waters of the eastern Pacific are very different from those in the Caribbean. The two faunas, having evolved independently of each other for millions of years while separated by the intervening Panamanian isthmus, would now be mingled by currents flooding from the Pacific side. Among the many unfortunate likely results would be the invasion of the Caribbean waters by poisonous sea snakes as well as by sea wasps, a form of stinging jellyfish.

A second example of national impetuosity I happened to witness was the U.S. Department of Agriculture's fire ant eradication program. Rachel Carson was to label it, in *Silent Spring*, "an outstanding example of an ill-conceived, badly executed, and thoroughly detrimental experiment in the mass control of insects, an experiment so expensive in dollars, in destruction of animal life, and in loss of public confidence in the Agriculture Department that it is incomprehensible that any funds should still be devoted to it."

The target of this fiasco was the red imported fire ant (*Solenopsis invicta*), which had been introduced into the port of Mobile, Alabama, most likely in cargo shipped from Argentina. Its colonies, each containing several hundred thousand very aggressive workers, construct soil nests surmounted by mounds as much as a foot high. The name fire ant comes from its sting, which feels like a burning match held too close to the skin. The exact time of the establishment of the species in the United States is not known but was probably sometime in the 1930s. By rare coincidence I was the first person unofficially to record its presence. In 1942, as a thirteen-year-old Boy Scout studying ant species around my home near the Mobile docks, I discovered a single well-developed colony of red imported fire ants. Seven years later, when the species had become abundant enough to rank as a local pest, I was hired by the state of Alabama to make the first thorough study of its habits and distribution. I found that the ants were spreading radially outward from Mobile at the rate of about five miles a year and had already reached the borders of Florida and Mississippi. By continuing this advance, and also by hitchhiking in nursery and farm products, they were destined to spread during the next several decades throughout the South from the Carolinas to Texas.

The red imported fire ant was and remains a serious nuisance. Its stings are unpleasant, and on rare occasions the venom triggers fatal anaphylactic shock. The teeming workers have been known to attack seedling corn and other crops as well as the hatchlings of ground-nesting birds. Its mounds are large and numerous enough to interfere with the operation of farm machinery. Yet it was never an economic pest in the same class as the boll weevil, gypsy moth, European corn borer, and other destructive insects.

Its conspicuous and menacing behavior nevertheless caused enough alarm for the U.S. Department of Agriculture, with enthusiastic support from the pesticide industry, to launch an eradication effort, not just to control the ant but to remove it entirely from American soil. In 1958 a million acres were sprayed with the powerful insecticides dieldrin and heptachlor. As Rachel Carson documented in *Silent Spring*, the environmental results were catastrophic. Wildlife and livestock exposed to the poisons, through direct contact or in polluted water, began to suffer an often fatal nervous disorder. Many bird populations were decimated. The effects on human health were never assessed, and the probably destructive elements on native insect populations — those elements necessary for the healthy functioning of the natural ecosystems — were hardly mentioned.

The red imported fire ants bounded back after the pesticide carpet bombing and continued their spread across the South without pause. This disconcerting outcome was easy to predict. In the genetic strain of the red imported fire ant then prevalent, each colony is started by a single mated queen and grows to maturity within one to three years. At that point it starts to generate thousands of new queens, each capable of traveling for miles in the air before settling down to start a new colony. Just one surviving colony missed by the poison sprays is enough to reseed an area of many square miles. When a new formal scientific name was later picked for the species (to clear up a confusion in its taxonomic history), the logical choice was *invicta*, meaning "unconquered." By the late 1960s, as the eradication effort wound down, I felt justified in calling the campaign against the unconquered ant the "Vietnam of Entomology."

Rachel Carson, in recounting such horror stories in *Silent Spring*, did not call for an end to pest control. Rather, she asked for an end to reckless endangerment by the use of broad-spectrum pesticides. These substances, she argued, should never be spread across the nation's fruited plains without adequate and public knowledge of their impact on the environment and human health. Instead, she insisted, we must switch to clean, precise solutions based on science and broad environmental knowledge.

For the most part, Americans listened and began to turn away from wholesale toxic pollution. The Carson ethic spread to other countries and to other venues within each country. It is not possible exactly to assess the full influence of *Silent Spring* on American environmentalism. In the decades that followed, the book's message was blended with other scientific and literary efforts and folded into the growing activist movement, which was drawn from multiple social and political agendas. But whatever the genealogy, no one can deny that Rachel Carson's book exerted, and continues to exert, a major influence. In immediate impact, it accelerated the resistance to chemical pollution that is all but universal today — in word if not always in deed. *Silent Spring* also became a national political force, largely responsible for the establishment of the Environmental Protection Agency in 1970. The task of pesticide oversight and the Food Safety Inspection Service were transferred to the new agency from the Department of Agriculture, marking a turnabout in policy emphasis from the benefits of chemical crop treatments to their risks.

A collateral effect of *Silent Spring* was the boost it gave to conservation of natural environments. Chemical pollution is the third-ranking cause of species extinction in the United States, after habitat destruction and "biological pollution" — the influx of alien species that outcompete and push back native ones. The general environmental concern abetted by *Silent Spring* resulted in the passage in 1973 of the Endangered Species Act by a near-unanimous vote in Congress. In concept and effect the act is easily the most important piece of conservation legislation in the nation's history. Its most dramatic successes include the recovery of the American alligator, gray whale, bald eagle, peregrine falcon, and eastern population of the brown pelican. All were imperiled forty years ago, and all are now considered relatively safe.

The environmental movement nevertheless is still forced to work its way up the rough side of the mountain, even in the country that gave it birth. If Rachel Carson were alive today, I believe she would give America a mixed grade. The increased public awareness of the environment would please the educator in her; the ranking of her book as a literary classic would astonish the writer; and the existence of new regulatory laws would gratify the frustrated government bureaucrat. The naturalist in Rachel Carson, positioned at the core of her several parts, would take pleasure in knowing that ecocidal schemes such as the sea-level canal and the fire ant eradication program, if broached today, would be widely ridiculed and perish stillborn.

Even so, she would recognize that the war between environmentalists and exploiters, local and national, is far from over. It has only subsided since 1962 to a more muted equilibrium. Although developers and policymakers come up with fewer spectacularly bad large projects, they continue to chip, saw, and drill away at the remains of the American natural environment. They say, over and over, we just need a little more here and there. The environmentalists respond by saying, pull back: nature is dying the torture-death of a thousand cuts.

Of the 1,254 species protected under the Endangered Species Act at the end of 1991, four times as many are declining as are gaining in population. The enemies of federal environmental regulation cite this difference as evidence that the act has failed. Their logic, if applied widely, would call for closing hospital emergency rooms because so many people die there. They declare the Endangered Species Act a detriment to economic growth, conveniently ignoring the fact that fewer than one in a thousand projects reviewed under its provisions has been halted.

During the past forty years the United States has come to understand that it is a major player in the deterioration of the global environment. Rachel Carson, who was a quick learner, would be ahead of us in understanding the devastating effects everywhere of still-rocketing population growth combined with consumption of natural resources, the thinning of the ozone layer, global warming, the collapse of marine fisheries, and, less directly through foreign trade, the decimation of tropical forests and mass extinction of species. She would regret, I am sure, the sorry example the United States sets with its enormous per capita appropriation of productive land around the world for its consumption — ten times that of developing countries.

On the other hand, the lady from Maryland would take some hope from Earth Summit, the successful Montreal Protocol aimed at the reduction of ozone-thinning chlorofluorocarbons, and the less successful Kyoto Protocol designed to slow climatic warming (still thwarted in 2002 by lack of American approval). She would be cheered by news of the rapid growth in funding by the muscle of such global nongovernmental organizations as Conservation International, the Nature Conservancy, and the World Wildlife Fund–U.S.

Silent Spring continues to be worthy of our attention because it marks an important moment in history, just as Harriet Beecher Stowe's *Uncle Tom's Cabin* and John Muir's

Our National Parks do. The examples and arguments it contains are timeless lessons of the kind we need to reexamine. They are also timely, because the battle Rachel Carson helped to lead on behalf of the environment is far from won.

We are still poisoning the air and water and eroding the biosphere, albeit less so than if Rachel Carson had not written. Today we understand better than ever why we must press the effort to save the environment all the way home, true to the mind and spirit of the valiant author of *Silent Spring*.

JIM LYNCH

Rachel Carson in *The Highest Tide*

I DIDN'T SET out to pay homage to Rachel Carson with *The Highest Tide*. But after studying her oceanography books and learning about her life, I couldn't resist trying to weave her into my novel.

Like most people, I knew her for *Silent Spring*. And for that daring masterpiece alone, I considered her one of the wisest Americans ever. I didn't know her story. I didn't know that her first calling was oceanography or that she'd written three classics about the sea.

While researching my Puget Sound novel, I plowed through a dozen tedious marine biology books before discovering a used copy of *The Edge of the Sea* at Orca Books in Olympia, Washington. Standing aside the racks, I read the first chapter as if it were a letter Carson had mailed to me.

The timing, the prose, the context all felt serendipitous.

I was about to take an unpaid leave from my newspaper job to try to write a coming-of-age story steeped in the enchantment and mystery of the tidal world. And here was this manuscript by the great Rachel Carson with a first chapter that ends with the notion that our quest to understand the meaning of life inevitably draws us back to the salty beaches.

> It sends us back to the edge of the sea, where the drama of life played its first scene on earth and perhaps even its prelude; where the forces of evolution are at work today, as they have been since the appearance of what we know as life; and where the spectacle of living creatures faced by the cosmic realities of their world is crystal clear.

After savoring *The Edge of the Sea*, I devoured *The Sea Around Us* and was dazzled again by the fearless authority and grace with which Carson wrote: "There is no drop of water in the ocean, not even in the deepest parts of the abyss, that does not know and respond to the mysterious forces that create the tide."

She seemed as comfortable and insightful explaining the initial cooling of the planet as she was describing the desires of a solitary crab at the surf's edge at night. Just as endearing was her admission that she didn't have all the answers. She marveled at the inexplicable, such as the way salmon return to the exact creek they exited as babies or the way grunions sense the highest tide of the month and hurl themselves on the beach to mate in the sand.

Reading Carson's work raised the bar for me. Her descriptions of the sea were inspiring not only for their music but for their precision. And the gravity and fascination she brought to her writing bolstered my hopes of making the tidal world come alive on the page. She gave me confidence that I could use Puget Sound as more than a gorgeous backdrop, that I could actually plunk readers into its mud and knee-deep in its tide and make them experience it.

My novel took full flight once I decided to pass along my obsession with Carson's work to my protagonist, Miles, a thirteen-year-old loner so observant of the marine world that he is in the best position to connect the dots when a succession of mysterious and exotic sea life washes up near his home one summer.

I worried, initially, that it would feel like a stretch. Why would a modern teenage boy swoon over the writings of a woman scientist from the 1950s? But the more I learned about Carson and the more I thought about Miles, the more sense it made.

Carson was, like Miles, a passionate beachcomber at her core. And she too was somewhat of a hyperobservant loner as well as an underdog — a mid-twentieth-century middle-aged woman who dared to educate the masses on the interconnectedness of life. However, what clinched it for me was her last book, *The Sense of Wonder.*

That wise little book, and its ambitious goal of instilling in children a permanent instinct "for what is beautiful and awe-inspiring," convinced me that Miles embodies the sense of curiosity and amazement that Carson wished we all could sustain.

Unfortunately, in some ways I am afraid that I wrote a time capsule. Reader reactions have made it clear that it is increasingly rare for teenagers to possess the desire or the freedom to immerse themselves in nature the way Miles does. While digesting that feedback, I came across Richard Louv's *Last Child in the Woods*, in which he asserts the persuasive premise that many children today are suffering from nature-deficit disorder.

If Carson were still around, I suspect that she would be thrilled that such a high percentage of children seem to understand that we need to protect the environment, but she would likely be worried that a shrinking percentage of kids actually experience it or have any personal relationship with it.

Regardless, one of the rewards of publishing *The Highest Tide* has been the opportunity to discuss Carson with readers. While many younger readers have never heard of her, many others recall her books fondly, even reverentially. And plenty of readers have thanked me for reconnecting them to her, as if she were their long-lost friend or mentor. It continues to please me to hear booksellers say that they have stockpiled her books at the request of *Highest Tide* fans.

Mostly though, I am simply indebted to Carson for her inspiration and honored by her presence in my novel, from its first to its final pages.

From The Highest Tide

Two days later, the low tide was a minus-three, and when the water dropped a yard lower than usual in Chatham Cove additional football fields of mud, gravel and sea life unfurled, tripling our chances of seeing something unusual or finding large clams.

See, Professor Kramer had helped me get a specimen collector's agreement and a commercial clamming license from the state. So if I found marketable clams I sold them to the owner of the Saigon Secret. And when it came to digging up the largest, most deeply burrowed clams around, I usually called on the long arms of Kenny Phelps.

Phelps was a month younger and a head taller than me with a lazy swagger and long brown bangs that hid his right eye whenever he looked down. "Fuck-you bangs" is what he called them. His favorite pastime was air guitar, but unlike the rest of us, he took it seriously. When he mimicked Hendrix, for example, he'd flip over his imaginary guitar and play it upside down and left-handed. Another thing about him: He was a slacker. His philosophy was that the best jobs involved the least amount of work. His favorite scam? Going door to door offering to clean roofs and gutters in the fall. The beauty of it, he explained, was that homeowners couldn't watch him work. If he said it took two hours then it took two hours, even if one and a half were spent huddled near the chimney puffing Kent Menthol 100s he stole from his mother. And Phelps was clever with a cigarette. He loved to pop off large smoke rings, then squeeze three little ones right through them whenever he had an audience. The only thing screwing up his bad-boy act was his long, friendly smile that came so easily he could've held it for those old, slow cameras and still looked natural.

Phelps wanted me to pay him by the hour, including a half-hour lunch and two fifteen-minute smoke breaks every three hours. His stepdad was big in the electricians' union, and Phelps liked to throw union standards and slogans at me. I offered him half of whatever we earned, which was nothing some days, days he likened to slavery. Why'd I put up with him? I wasn't superchummy with anyone my age. My best friend was old Florence, and she never left her cabin and was getting sicker by the week. Phelps was convenient. He was the closest kid to the bay, so summers tossed us together. Plus, his gangly arms and long, strong fingers were built for clamming.

We started out studying the little chimney holes in the mud through which clams siphoned and spat seawater, hunting for the telltale signs of the mighty geoduck. Most of those huge clams — pronounced *gooey-duck* for some reason — lived farther out in the bay, but there were still plenty of exposed burrows if the tide fell low enough and you knew where to look.

As usual, we were the only ones out there. Most clammers and beachcombers headed north to rockier shores where tidal life was supposedly more abundant even though our southern bays endured the biggest tidal swings in the

West, with water levels fluctuating as much as twenty feet in six hours. Still, South Sound had a reputation for mass-producing sand dollars and little else. The people behind those theories apparently never spent any time on Chatham Cove. The assumption was the Squaxins owned it, but actually just a slice of the flats belonged to the tribe, which was pointed out to me by Judge Stegner, who owned a slice himself. The state owned the rest, and from what I could tell, Chatham and the shoals north of it gathered new species of stars, snails, crabs, worms, or jellies on a weekly basis — not that Phelps noticed.

While we searched for figure-eight depressions, he updated me on Wendy Pratto's breasts. He'd seen her in Safeway and swore her hooters were already a size bigger than they were the last day of school. "I'm guessing they're thirty-four Cs, now," he said authoritatively.

He stooped, pinched loose a tip of root-beer-colored kelp, chewed it to shreds then spat it out. He'd initially tried to con me into paying him to taste beach life, then did it to amuse himself. It became a habit. He nibbled on sea lettuce and eel grass. He ate baby shrimp and manilas straight from the shell. I saw him corner and catch a baby sculpin in a tide pool and swallow that one-inch fish whole. He gave me the latest on Christy Decker's chest too, claiming he'd seen it rise from the YMCA pool with nipples he could've hung his bathrobe on.

It wasn't that I didn't notice the same girls, but to me they were as remote and two-dimensional as movie stars. If I couldn't talk to them, they didn't enter my fantasies. I could talk to Angie Stegner — even if I didn't always make sense.

The pale two-thirds moon still hung in the sky, and for some reason I chose that moment to inform Phelps that Rachel Carson believed the moon was originally a glob of earth that ripped loose from the bottom of the Pacific and spun into the sky while the planet was still cooling.

"She also said the gravitational pull from the moon causes friction that is gradually slowing the earth's spin. So while it now takes twenty-four hours for it to rotate, it will eventually take fifty times that long. You imagine living in a world that has the equivalent of fifty straight days of light followed by fifty days of darkness?"

Phelps glared up at me from our clam ditch through those fuck-you bangs. "You're a freak," he said. "Why don't you use all your homo-reading to study something of value to us?"

"Like what?"

"Like the G-spot."

"The what?"

"The G-spot, Squid Boy." Phelps popped out a Kent, clutched it between the least dirty of his fingers and lit it. "It's the button inside women that drives them wild." He mumbled around his cigarette like a gangster. "Once we find out where it's at, we're *in.*"

I was baffled. I'd never heard about any secret control panel inside women.

"Let's see your fingers," Phelps said.

I reluctantly stuck out my hand. He frowned. "I think they're too short."

"For what?"

"To reach the button. My brother says you need a finger that's at least two and a half inches long. Either that or you've gotta get your pecker to bend upwards."

I thought about my pecker. If anything it bent slightly to the left. "How're you supposed to do that?"

He glared at me as if I were his slowest student. "Concentration," he said knowingly.

"You're full of crap," I said. "Your brother is messing with you again."

"Whatever you say, Squid Boy."

"I say, keep digging."

The G-spot? It definitely hadn't come up in sex ed. In fact, there was nothing sexy about sex ed. All I got from it was the unsettling understanding that my life was a ridiculous long shot. First, my mother had to be flattered by my father while waiting impatiently for meatball subs at Meconi's. Then one particular sperm cell of his eighteen zillion sperm cells had to elude whatever *goalie* — my father's term — they were using. (I'd overheard my mother call me "an accident" at least seven times.) Then that blind, microscopic sperm of his had to find and crack that one particular moody egg of hers during that vague window of time it was available without later getting aborted by some bald, distracted doctor who was thinking about the Mariners' bullpen at the time. What were the odds? I was a fluke in a classroom full of flukes on a planet overpopulated by flukes.

A while later, I caught Phelps glancing at the moon, the closest thing to a cloud up there. "When did Rachel Carson write all that stuff?" he asked.

"Early nineteen-fifties."

"How old was she?"

"Her late forties."

"When'd she die?"

"Nineteen sixty-four."

"What of?"

"Breast cancer."

"How many books she write?"

"Four. All bestsellers. She was the one who warned us that if we keep spraying poisons on fields we'll stop hearing birds in the spring."

"How many kids she have?"

"None. Never married."

"You know everything about her, don't you?"

I didn't say anything for a couple beats. "I know she was brave and brilliant."

"Know what I know?" Phelps couldn't control his smile. "I know you're in love with a spinster who's been dead for decades."

"Keep digging."

Phelps eventually dug up a seven-pound geoduck that would convert into three and a half bucks for each of us. If you haven't seen a geoduck before you'd be astonished. They're not the clams you know. Their shells are ridiculously undersized. Even when contracted, their necks hang way out. Think of bodybuilders in Speedos, or as Professor Kramer himself put it, there's no getting around their resemblance to horse dicks.

When I helped the professor explain the tidal flats to third-graders it was always hard to get them past the giggles to make them understand that as silly as geoducks look, they possess one of the most durable designs on earth. They bury themselves two feet deep in sand, then shove their oversized necks up through the sea floor where they can comfortably inhale plankton and spit out waste for a century or more. By the time I'd tell them that the biggest ones swell to twenty pounds and live up to 150 years without ever having to move, I'd be talking to myself.

The tide was returning quicker than I'd expected, sneaking up on me the way it did when my mind drifted. So instead of digging flooding burrows, I waded, hunting for anything the big aquariums might want, wishing I'd started searching earlier instead of wasting time trying to educate someone as thickheaded as Phelps.

I told him to help me turn rocks before they submerged, hoping to find baby octopus, reminding him to put the rocks back exactly the way he found them. A few minutes later, I saw five toothpick-legged sandpipers scissor-stepping across the flats in such choreographed precision I half-expected them to start twirling canes and whistling in unison. Then I heard Phelps shriek.

By the time I looked his way, he was already tripping backward onto compact sand. That part wasn't unusual.

Phelps rarely went a day without hurting himself. Who else broke his collarbone bowling or sprained his neck sneezing? But this time he was reeling and screeching, as if chased. "It snapped at me!"

I knew what he'd seen before I got to the rock he'd flipped.

Midshipmen rank among the Sound's creepiest bottom fish. Their bodies are mostly heads, and their heads are mostly eyes and teeth. And for whatever reason, the females rise up from the dark canyons to drop their eggs beneath rocks in the shallows. The males then guard the eggs until they hatch, and if you startle them they'll show you their piranhalike teeth. After this daddy showed me his, I saw tiny eggs adhered to the underside of the upturned rock and the baby midshipmen spinning inside them, their metallic stripes creating a sparkling light show. I waved Phelps over.

He stood hesitantly behind me as the flashing babies popped from their eggs and splashed into two inches of water where they huddled against their father's belly. Then the tumult passed and they all became so still, the babies seemingly disappearing, the father blending into the rocks.

"Now *that*," Phelps whispered, "is amazing."

"Look around." I held out my hands, as if catching rain.

SANDRA STEINGRABER

Silent Spring: A Father-Daughter Dance

IN *THE YEAR OF MAGICAL THINKING*, Joan Didion says that "there comes a point at which we must relinquish the dead, let them go, keep them dead. Let them become the photograph on the table. Let them become the name on the trust accounts." It's an astonishing concession, coming as it does near the end of a book that chronicles the various psychic methods that the author deployed, in her first year of widowhood, to make her deceased spouse not dead. It is the surrender we had watched her fend off over and over in previous chapters and so forms a turning point in this documentary of grief.

I did not lose my father to sudden cardiac arrest at the dinner table, as Didion lost her husband, John. I lost him to a neurological illness — Lewy body dementia — that unfolded over twenty years. Or more. It's hard to know.

While Didion was obsessed with determining precisely when her husband's life ended — at the table? in the ambulance? at the hospital? — I was obsessed, after my father's death, with figuring out when his dying started. When precisely did dementia first sink its teeth into my father's brain? When he cut down the hedges in front of his house because a stranger might hide there, was that the disease? Almost certainly. When he summarily refused to meet my college boyfriend on Christmas Eve eight years earlier, was that the disease? Not clear. Maybe it was the boyfriend. How about that time Dad purchased five chain saws because they were on sale? Well, he always liked a bargain. So maybe that was just Dad. But even before chain saws, he stopped answering the telephone. And that must have been the disease.

Didion resisted the objectification of her departed partner. She longed for him to return — not turn into the picture on the table. I, however, yearned for my father to become something inanimate, to turn into some beloved thing that I could remember him by. And I did this, I now admit, even before he died. Even before the police and the involuntary admission to the psychiatric hospital, when Dad was still at home, monitoring the troop movements of ants on the porch and talking about wartime Italy.

It was a fantasy I indulged during the later years when Dad was in the nursing home and I would visit Mom at the house. I would walk through the rooms that he had designed and built for his young bride in 1956 and where I had grown up. He was not there. He was not there in the yard or the porch or the garden or the garage. But he was not dead either. He was in an underworld where I could check in on him periodically by punching a secret code (zero-one-six-star) into an electronic panel that controlled the locked doors of the Alzheimer's unit. There, amid the muttering and ranting of the unit's other residents, I could touch him and smell him and attend to him. Sometimes he knew me. Sometimes he did not. Sometimes he would ask me for a ticket home, and I would resist the impulse to slip him the code for the doors. Once I tried to usher him into the courtyard where there were flowerbeds, benches, and stone paths, but the colors were too bright, too confusing. He fell to his knees and covered his eyes. He threw gravel at the nurses who came to help us. That was his last encounter with sunlight.

After that visit — and others like it — I came back to the house, where Dad was not, and I would imagine that he was not just absent but really and truly gone — dead, unvisitable, unattendable — and that I possessed something inanimate in his place, something he had lovingly bequeathed to me.

The object I imagined as my father's replacement was a copy of *Silent Spring. His* copy: a battered paperback with simple black lettering and a line drawing of a stream meandering diagonally across the cover. The one he had used as a course textbook in the consumer education class he taught. *Silent Spring* was an unusual choice for such a class

— especially in the early 1960s — but that was part of my point to myself. His choice of that book meant that he was once a creative, clever, forward-thinking man, a thoughtful educator. And if I held that copy of *Silent Spring* in my hands — so I imagined — the childhood memory of my father as smart, capable, caring, and gentle would push away the adult memory of my father as delusional, violent, paranoid, and crazy.

I myself had a battered copy of *Silent Spring* in my library, along with many newer editions, and, as far as I know, my father may even have given it to me years before. But the copy I wanted was his old green one — I had never seen another one like it, actually — because that is the one he pulled from his briefcase each afternoon when he walked home from teaching.

1963. I am four years old. I watch out the window of the north-facing bedroom, looking for the legs of my father to appear beneath the tree branches at the curve of the road. There's Dad! I'm allowed to run outside and greet him. He twirls me around. We walk back home together. I ask if any of the girls in his class had fancy hairdos today. He laughs and says no. I follow him to the couch. He opens his briefcase and lays a book on the coffee table. I can't read yet, but I know the book by the green cover. Silent Spring. *The book that the grownups all talk about. Because of the drawing on the cover, I believe that the book is about a spring of water. Not until graduate school do I realize the title refers to the death of songbirds. Not to the silence of aquifers.*

When my father was living in the nursing home, I had poked around in his big desk to see if the old green *Silent Spring* might be tucked away somewhere — his home office had been turned into the guest room — but I didn't find it quickly, and it felt wrong to keep looking. It wasn't on the bookshelf in the dining room either. Maybe there was no green book.

1970. My sister and I sit behind a tippy card table at the end of the driveway. The table is loaded with garden produce. Behind us a sign hand-lettered by our father announces ORGANIC TOMATOES 25 CENTS/POUND. *It's a big day for us. Dad has equipped Julie and me with a change box and will let us keep the profits from the sale of his vegetables. Cars stop. Some people want to know what* organic *means. My sister and I explain. We describe the ladybugs and praying mantises my father receives by mail order to serve as natural predators for the pests that other gardeners might spray with pesticides. We talk about our father's compost pile. We talk about his mulch. Some customers still don't understand. What's the matter with them? Maybe Dad should come out and tell them about* Silent Spring. *Dad knows everything.*

Two years after my father died, I came home with my five-year-old son for the wedding of a childhood friend. Mom gave us the north-facing room, my old bedroom. While hanging my bridesmaid dress in the closet, I pushed a box of books out of the way and accidentally tipped it over. And there it was. Pale green cover with a black line drawing.

Silent Spring. Just as I had remembered. It was part of a limited special edition that the Consumers' Union made available to its members in 1962. Dexter Masters, then its executive director, had written the foreword. No wonder I had never seen another copy like it. I had found the book that united my life with my father's. It was the text that had changed both of our lives.

For my father, *Silent Spring* was an antidote to wartime thinking. Dad had served as a teenage soldier in Naples where the pesticide DDT was first deployed to halt a typhus epidemic. The motto of his antitank unit — seek, strike, and destroy — might as well have been the advertising slogan for DDT and other pesticides that had been developed for use in warfare and then were aggressively marketed to farmers, housewives, and suburban homeowners after the war ended. Returning GIs were urged to grab a bottle of poison and go after dandelions, mosquitoes, and grubs. In demonizing the home front's new enemy, one ad even went so far as to place Adolf Hitler's head onto the body of a beetle.

My father had no stomach for waging war in his backyard. The garden was a respite from command and control. It was a place for puttering, experimenting, and nurturing. He enjoyed learning about nonchemical techniques of pest control and trying new tricks he'd read about in gardening magazines. He revered praying mantises and ladybugs. To him, organic gardening was enlightened, scientific, and sensible. So when Rachel Carson said things like "The 'control of nature' is a phrase conceived in arrogance, born of the Neanderthal age of biology and the convenience of man" her message resonated with my father. *Silent Spring* was his armistice.

1971. Dad stops taking walks in the evening. The gathering of twilight apparently reminds him of guard duty. Walking past houses where lights are flicking on is frightening to him, Mom says. Especially upsetting are the glimpses of women cooking dinner as framed by the yellow squares of kitchen windows. Such scenes make him fear that he will be compelled to walk all night. Armed. Under orders. Past civilian checkpoints. Anyone could be the enemy. Was that the disease? Or was that my dad?

No, that was the war.

1972. I should be helping Dad water the fruit trees, but instead I am lying on the porch reading a long historical novel. It's so hot and humid the back of my legs leave pools of sweat on the plastic of the reclining lawn chair. Dad walks up from the garden. I can feel the heat pouring from his body as he approaches. His right hand is curled into a fist, which he holds out to me. "Hold out your hand," he says. His eyes twinkle. He uncurls his fingers and spills into my palm a black stream of berries. "The first boysenberries," he whispers rhapsodically, and watches me taste a few. They are sweet and sun-warm and taste faintly of salt from his hands. They are beyond delicious. My evident pleasure makes him smile. "You eat some, too," I urge. "No, those are all for you, sweetheart," he says, and walks into the house. That was my dad. That was not the disease.

For me, who did not actually read the book until I was a college professor myself, *Silent Spring* was the reason I left the laboratory and became a science writer. By the late 1980s, Rachel Carson had been resurrected as the patron saint of a newly radicalizing breast cancer movement. Taking a lesson from the AIDS activists of the mid-1980s — who had done so much to redirect scientific research down paths of inquiry that held the most promise for saving lives — breast cancer activists began demanding more research into cancer prevention and toward explaining the environmental links to the disease. Carson's own hidden life as a breast cancer patient was part of her allure for breast cancer activists. Here was a scientist who had not only assembled formidable evidence for the harm of pesticides but who had done so while undergoing chemotherapy herself. Here was a scientist who, without even the assistance of a cancer registry or a toxics-release inventory, had correctly documented an increase in the prevalence of human cancers that corresponded with the rapid chemicalization of our economy after World War II.

The early 1990s redefined breast cancer awareness to include environmental awareness. Women at breast cancer rallies took to waving copies of *Silent Spring* as they marched. As a young biologist and also a cancer survivor, I became interested. Prompted by an invitation to speak about Rachel Carson's life as a cancer patient, I finally read *Silent Spring*, the book that served as the constant stage prop of my childhood. I read it again. I read it again and again. I visited Carson's archives at the Beinecke Library at Yale. I began corresponding with Carson's biographer

Linda Lear, who, at the time, was in the thick of her own research and writing.

As an environmental biologist, I was already impressed with the evidence that was beginning to pile up in the scientific literature about the various links between toxic chemical exposure and human health problems. As a cancer patient, I was aware that very little of this evidence was presented to the public. I began to wonder if I could write books that, like *Silent Spring*, constructed a bridge over that breach. I knew I had access to records on cancer incidence, birth defect prevalence, toxic releases, and pesticide sprayings that had not been available to Carson. And I had picked up a master's degree in creative writing before I had started my graduate work in biology. I had been a biologist by day and a poet by night. But perhaps there was a way of bridging this breach as well.

I found myself rereading Carson's acknowledgments at the beginning of *Silent Spring*. She credits citizen activists as much as scientists for making her work possible. "In a letter written in January 1958, Olga Owens Huckins told me of her own bitter experience of a small world made lifeless and so brought my attention sharply back to a problem with which I had long been concerned. I then realized I must write this book." And there was also this from a 1958 letter Carson wrote to Dorothy Freeman: "Knowing what I do, there would be no future peace for me if I kept silent."

1993. I have left my job in Chicago and moved to Boston, where, with the help of a postdoctoral fellowship at Harvard, I hope to begin writing a book that will examine environmental links to human cancers. The day after my arrival, I attend a political rally organized by breast cancer activists. Someone hands me a sign to carry. At that very moment, a photographer from the Boston Herald *snaps my picture. The next day, the newspaper runs a quarter-page photo of me squinting resolutely into the sun and holding a placard that reads* RACHEL CARSON WAS RIGHT! *I would like to send the clip to my father, but he is, at this point, too demented to understand it.*

No, he is not. The truth is that I am fearful of his disapproval. For my father, Rachel Carson is less Che Guevara and more Charles Darwin, quietly and objectively amassing evidence and presenting it before a curious public. A lifelong Republican, he did not associate the demure and dignified Carson with protest marches, for which he has little patience. That was just Dad. Not the disease. *Silent Spring* was my father's armistice. It was my call to arms.

Recently, I have become fascinated by the evident reciprocity between environmental activism and *Silent Spring*. Carson was as influenced by activism and advocacy as the contemporary environmental movement was influenced — some would say inaugurated — by the publication of *Silent Spring*. If I'm right about this, it means the popular portrait of Carson as a lone, impartial, above-the-fray genius requires some revision.

Let's take another look at Olga Owens Huckins, the letter-writer Carson credits with providing the raison d'être for *Silent Spring*. As is painstakingly documented in Lear's biography *Rachel Carson: Witness for Nature*, Huckins was more than simply a concerned citizen pleading with Carson to investigate the ecological effects of pesticides. Huckins was an organic gardener, an editor, and a member of the Committee Against Mass Poisoning, which sought, through lawsuits and protests, to halt the aerial spraying of pesticides. Throughout 1957, members of this committee, including Huckins, wrote letters to the editors of many New England and Long Island newspapers. These letters did not scientifically document the harm created by the widespread use of pesticides. Instead, they bore witness to many small tragedies, such as dead birds piling up around backyard birdbaths in the aftermath of a particular spraying episode. These letters were also quite polemical. From one: "Stop the spraying of poisons everywhere until all the evidence, biological and scientific, immediate and long run, of the effects upon wildlife and human beings is known."

The Committee Against Mass Poisoning took a human rights approach to environmental harm — as contemporary environmental justice advocates continue to do. In the parlance of today's environmental activists, the introduction of harmful chemicals into air, food, and water (and thereby into our bodies) violates the right to privacy as well as security of person and is referred to as an act of "toxic trespass." Likewise, Huckins condemned aerial spraying of pesticides as "inhumane, undemocratic, and probably unconstitutional."

The citizen lawsuit filed by the committee was particularly useful to Carson because, as it wended its way to the

Supreme Court, it became a magnet for media attention. Carson was thus able to elicit the interest of essayist E. B. White about the lawsuit, and White in turn piqued the interest of *The New Yorker* editor William Shawn. When Shawn offered Carson fifty thousand words in *The New Yorker*, she knew she was on her way to writing a book.

In short, environmental activism in the 1950s opened up a critical space in the publishing industry for environmental writing, and that development, as much as the slow accumulation of scientific knowledge, was the genesis of *Silent Spring*.

2004. I give a copy of Amy Ehrlich's exquisite picture book Rachel: The Story of Rachel Carson *to my six-year-old daughter. I tell her that Papa is a great admirer of Rachel and that I am, too. We read it together. The page that describes the writing of* Silent Spring *features a picture of a tiny crab alone on a vast moonlit beach. These are the accompanying words: "When the book came out, the companies that made the poisons attacked it. And they attacked Rachel, too. She was only a woman, after all, emotional and unreliable. But other people believed her. They argued back and forth in the newspapers, on television, and in Washington. Committees were formed in Congress to investigate the poisons. Rachel dealt with both sides calmly, knowing she'd done all that she could. She was like a tiny, nearly transparent ghost crab she'd once written about, alone on a beach at night, facing the roaring surf."*

Dad would like that description. I'm not sure I do.

* * *

Two years after my father's death, alone in my old bedroom after returning home from the wedding, I sank down to the closet floor, opened the green tattered cover, and began reading. These were the very pages that my father's hands had once turned. I waited for the long-anticipated sense of relief to descend. It did not. Instead, the more I read, the more I missed my father. I wanted him to return to me — not as the smart, caring, organic gardener of my childhood nor as the confused, deluded stick figure of my adulthood, but as someone I had never known: a thoughtful adult companion to whom I could address my thoughtful adult questions.

Like this one, for example. Dad, take a look. On the one hand, Carson dedicates the book "To Albert Schweitzer who said 'Man has lost the capacity to foresee and to forestall. He will end by destroying the earth.'" On the other hand, she seems to disavow such fatalism in the acknowledgments that follow, where she predicts that citizen activism will rescue us from ruination: "Finally, I must acknowledge our vast indebtedness to a host of people . . . who first spoke out against the reckless and irresponsible poisoning of the world that man shares with all other creatures, and who are even now fighting the thousands of small battles that in the end will bring victory for sanity and common sense in our accommodation to the world that surrounds us."

So which is it, do you think, Dad? Destruction? Or victory?

The room my father built filled with silence.

AL GORE

Rachel Carson and *Silent Spring*

IN 1962, WHEN *Silent Spring* was first published, "environment" was not even an entry in the vocabulary of public policy. In a few cities, especially Los Angeles, smog had become a cause of concern, albeit more because of its appearance than because of its threat to public health. Conservation — the precursor of environmentalism — had been mentioned during the 1960 Democratic and Republican conventions, but only in passing and almost entirely in the context of national parks and natural resources. And except for a few scattered entries in largely inaccessible scientific journals, there was virtually no public dialogue about the growing, invisible dangers of DDT and other pesticides and chemicals. *Silent Spring* came as a cry in the wilderness, a deeply felt, thoroughly researched, and brilliantly written argument that changed the course of history. Without this book, the environmental movement might have been long delayed or never have developed at all.

Not surprisingly, both the book and its author, who had once worked as a marine biologist for the Fish and Wildlife Service, met with considerable resistance from those who were profiting from pollution. Major chemical companies tried to suppress *Silent Spring*, and when excerpts appeared in *The New Yorker*, a chorus of voices immediately accused Carson of being hysterical and extremist — charges still heard today whenever anyone questions those whose financial well-being depends on maintaining the environmental status quo. (Having been labeled "Ozone Man" during the 1992 presidential campaign, a name that was probably not intended as a compliment but that I wore as a badge of honor, I am aware that raising these issues invariably inspires a fierce — and sometimes foolish — reaction.) By the time the book became widely available, the forces arrayed against its author were formidable.

The attack on Rachel Carson has been compared to the bitter assault on Charles Darwin when he published *The Origin of Species*. Moreover, because Carson was a woman, much of the criticism directed at her played on stereotypes of her sex. Calling her "hysterical" fit the bill exactly. *Time* magazine added the charge that she had used "emotion-fanning words." She was dismissed by others as "a priestess of nature." Her credibility as a scientist was attacked as well: opponents financed the production of propaganda that supposedly refuted her work. It was all part of an intense, well-financed negative campaign, not against a political candidate but against a book and its author.

Carson brought two decisive strengths to this battle: a scrupulous respect for the truth and a remarkable degree of personal courage. She had checked and rechecked every paragraph in *Silent Spring*, and the passing years have revealed that her warnings were, if anything, understated. And her courage, which matched her vision, went far beyond her willingness to disturb an entrenched and profitable industry. While writing *Silent Spring*, she endured a radical mastectomy and then radiation treatment. Two years after the book's publication, she died, of breast cancer. Ironically, new research points strongly to a link between this disease and exposure to toxic chemicals. So in a sense, Carson was literally writing for her life.

She was also writing against the grain of an orthodoxy rooted in the earliest days of the scientific revolution: that man (and of course this meant the male of our species) was properly the center and the master of all things, and that scientific history was primarily the story of his dominion — ultimately, it was hoped, to a nearly absolute state. When a woman dared to challenge this orthodoxy, one of its prominent defenders, Robert White Stevens, replied in terms that now sound not only arrogant but as quaint as the flat-earth theory: "The crux, the fulcrum over which the argument chiefly rests, is that Miss Carson maintains that the balance of nature is a major force in the survival of man, whereas the modern chemist, the modern biologist and scientist, believes that man is steadily controlling nature."

The very absurdity of that world view from today's perspective indicates how revolutionary Rachel Carson was. Assaults from corporate interests were to be expected, but even the American Medical Association weighed in on the chemical companies' side. The man who discovered the insecticidal properties of DDT had, after all, been awarded the Nobel Prize.

But *Silent Spring* could not be stifled. Solutions to the problems it raised weren't immediate, but the book itself achieved enormous popularity and broad public support. In addition to presenting a convincing case, Carson had won both financial independence and public credibility with two previous bestsellers, *The Sea Around Us* and *The Edge of the Sea*. Also, *Silent Spring* was published in the early years of a decade that was anything but silent, a decade when Americans were perhaps far readier than they had been to hear and heed the book's message. In a sense, the woman and the moment came together.

Eventually, both the government and the public became involved — not just those who read the book, but those who read the news or watched television. As sales of *Silent Spring* passed the half-million mark, *CBS Reports* scheduled an hour-long program about it, and the network went ahead with the broadcast even when two major corporate sponsors withdrew their support. President Kennedy discussed the book at a press conference and appointed a special panel to examine its conclusions. When the panel reported its findings, its paper was an indictment of corporate and bureaucratic indifference and a validation of Carson's warnings about the potential hazards of pesticides. Soon thereafter, Congress began holding hearings and the first grassroots environmental organizations were formed.

Silent Spring planted the seeds of a new activism that has grown into one of the great popular forces of all time. When Rachel Carson died, in the spring of 1964, it was becoming clear that her voice would never be silenced. She had awakened not only our nation but the world. The publication of *Silent Spring* can properly be seen as the beginning of the modern environmental movement.

For me personally, *Silent Spring* had a profound impact. It was one of the books we read at home at my mother's insistence and then discussed around the dinner table. My sister and I didn't like every book that made it to that table, but our conversations about *Silent Spring* are a happy and vivid memory. Indeed, Rachel Carson was one of the reasons why I became so conscious of the environment and so involved with environmental issues. Her example inspired me to write *Earth in the Balance*, which, not coincidentally, was published by Houghton Mifflin, the company that stood by Carson through all the controversy and that has since earned a reputation for publishing many fine books about the environmental dangers facing our world. Her picture hangs on my office wall among those of the political leaders, the presidents, and the prime ministers. It has been there for years — and it belongs there. Carson has had as much or more effect on me than any of them, and perhaps than all of them together.

Both a scientist and an idealist, Carson was also a loner who listened, something that those in places of power so often fail to do. *Silent Spring* was conceived when she received a letter from a woman named Olga Owens Huckins in Duxbury, Massachusetts, telling her that DDT was killing birds. Today, because Carson's work led to a ban on DDT, some of the species that were her special concern — eagles and peregrine falcons, for example — are no longer at the edge of extinction. It may be that the human species, too, or at least countless human lives, will be saved because of the words she wrote.

No wonder the impact of *Silent Spring* has been compared to that of *Uncle Tom's Cabin.* Both rank among the rare books that have transformed our society. Yet there are important differences. Harriet Beecher Stowe dramatized an issue that was already on everyone's mind and at the center of a great public debate; she gave a human face to an already dominant national concern. The picture of slavery she drew moved the national conscience. As Abraham Lincoln said when he met her, at the height of the Civil War, "so you're the little lady who started this whole thing." In contrast, Rachel Carson warned of a danger that hardly anyone saw; she was trying to put an issue on the national agenda, not bear witness to one that was already there. In that sense, her achievement was harder won. Ironically, when she testified before Congress in 1963, Senator Abraham Ribicoff's welcome eerily echoed Lincoln's words of exactly a century before: "Miss Carson," he said, "you are the lady who started all this."

Another difference between the books goes to the heart of *Silent Spring*'s continuing relevance. Slavery could be, and was, ended in a few years, although it has taken another century and more to even begin to deal with its aftermath. But if slavery could be abolished with the stroke of a pen, chemical pollution could not. Despite the power of Carson's argument, despite actions like the banning of DDT in the United States, the environmental crisis has grown worse, not better. Since the publication of *Silent Spring*, pesticide use on farms alone has doubled to 1.1 billion tons a year, and production of these dangerous chemicals has increased by 400 percent. We have banned certain pesticides at home, but we still produce them and export them to other countries. This not only involves a readiness to profit by selling others a hazard we will not accept for ourselves; it also reflects an elemental failure to comprehend that the laws of science do not observe the boundaries of politics. Poisoning the food chain anywhere ultimately poisons the food chain everywhere.

In one of Carson's few speeches, and one of her last, to the Garden Club of America, she acknowledged that things could get worse before they got better: "These are large problems, and there is no easy solution." Yet she also warned that the longer we waited, the more risks we ran: "We are subjecting whole populations to exposure to chemicals which animal experiments have proved to be extremely poisonous and in many cases cumulative in their effect. These exposures now begin at or before birth and — unless we change our methods — will continue through the lifetime of those now living. No one knows what the results will be, because we have no previous experience to guide us." Since she made these remarks, we have unfortunately gained an abundance of experience, as rates of cancer and other diseases that may be related to pesticide use have soared. The difficulty is not that we have done nothing. We have done some important things, but we have not done nearly enough.

The Environmental Protection Agency was established in 1970, in large part because of the concerns and the consciousness that Rachel Carson had raised. Pesticide regulation and the Food Safety Inspection Service were moved to the new agency from the Agriculture Department, which naturally tended to see the advantages and not the dangers of using chemicals on crops. Since 1962, Congress has called for the establishment of review, registration, and information standards for pesticides — not once, but several times. But many of these standards have been ignored, postponed, and eroded. For example, when the Clinton-Gore administration took office, standards for protecting farm workers from pesticides were still not in place, even though the EPA had been "working on them" since the early 1970s. Broad-spectrum pesticides such as DDT have been replaced by narrow-spectrum pesticides of even higher toxicity, which have not been adequately tested and present equal or even greater risks.

For the most part, hardliners within the pesticide industry have succeeded in delaying the implementation of protective measures called for in *Silent Spring*. It is astonishing to see the cosseting this industry has been accorded in Congress over the years. The statute that regulates pesticides, fungicides, and rodenticides sets far looser standards than those that regulate food and drugs, and Congress intentionally made them more difficult to enforce. In setting safe levels of a pesticide, the government takes into account not only its toxicity but also the economic benefit it provides. This dubious process pits increased agricultural production (which might be obtained otherwise) against potential increases in cancer and neurological disease. Moreover, the process for removing a hazardous pesticide from the market generally takes five to ten years. New pesticides, even if they are very toxic, can win approval if they work just marginally better than existing ones.

In my view, this is nothing more than the regulatory equivalent of "Been down so long it looks like up to me." The present system is a Faustian bargain — we get short-term gain at the expense of long-term tragedy. And there is reason to believe that the short term can be very short indeed. Many pesticides do not cause the total number of pests to decline; they may do so at first, but the pests eventually adapt by mutation and the chemicals become useless. Furthermore, we have focused research on pesticide effects on adults and not on children, who are especially vulnerable to these chemicals. We have examined each pesticide in isolation, but scientists generally have not yet researched combinations, which are the potentially far more perilous reality encountered in our fields and pastures and streams. Essentially, what we have inherited is a system of laws and loopholes, deadlines and delays, facades that barely disguise a wholesale failure of policy.

Rachel Carson showed that the excessive use of pesticides was inconsistent with basic values; that at their worst, they create what she called "rivers of death," and at their best, they cause mild harm for relatively little long-term gain. Yet the honest conclusion is that in the twenty-two years since the publication of *Silent Spring*, the legal, regulatory, and political system has failed to respond adequately. Because Carson understood not only the environment but the very different world of politics, she anticipated one of the reasons for this failure. At a time when almost no one discussed the twin contaminations of special-interest money and influence, she referred in her Garden Club speech to the "advantage . . . given to those who seek to block remedial legislation." Foreshadowing the present debate about political reform, she even condemned the tax deduction for lobbying expenses that this administration has sought to repeal, pointing out that the deduction "means, to cite a specific example, that the chemical industry may now work at bargain rates to thwart future attempts at regulation. . . . The industry wishing to pursue its course without legal restraint is now actually subsidized in its efforts." In short, the problem of pesticides, which she brilliantly diagnosed, is perpetuated by the problem of politics, which she uncannily predicted. Cleaning up politics is essential to cleaning up pollution.

The years-long failure of one endeavor helps to explain the years-long failure of the other. The results are as undeniable as they are unacceptable. In 1992, 2.2 billion pounds of pesticides were used in this country — eight pounds for every man, woman, and child. Many of the pesticides in use are known to be quite carcinogenic; others work by poisoning the nervous and immune systems of insects, and perhaps of humans. Although we no longer have the doubtful benefits of one household product that Carson described — "We can polish our floors with a wax guaranteed to kill any insect that walks over it" — today pesticides are being used on more than 900,000 farms and in 69 million homes.

In 1988, the EPA reported that the ground water in thirty-two states was contaminated with seventy-four different agricultural chemicals, including one, the herbicide atrazine, that is classified as a potential human carcinogen. Seventy million tons a year are used on cornfields in the Mississippi basin, and 1.5 million pounds of runoffs now flow into the drinking water of 20 million people. Atrazine is not removed by municipal water treatment; in springtime, the amount of atrazine in the water often exceeds the standards set by the Safe Drinking Water Act. In 1993, that was true for 25 percent of all the surface water in the entire Mississippi basin.

DDT and PCBs are virtually banned in the United States for other reasons, but pesticides that mimic the female hormone estrogen, which are close chemical cousins, are plentiful and are raising intense new concerns. Research from Scotland, Michigan, Germany, and elsewhere indicates that they lead to reduced fertility, testicular and breast cancer, and malformation of the genital organs. In the United States alone, as the tide of estrogen pesticides has crested in the past twenty years, the incidence of testicular cancer has risen by approximately 50 percent. The evidence also suggests that, for reasons not yet understood, there has recently been a worldwide drop in sperm counts of 50 percent. There is documented, irrefutable proof that these chemicals disrupt the reproductive capacity of wildlife. As three researchers concluded after reviewing the data for the *Journal of the Institute of Environmental Health Services*, "Today many wildlife populations are at risk." Many of these problems may be harbingers of vast and unpredictable changes in animal and human reproductive systems, but the pesticides' potentially harmful effects are not currently considered in regulatory risk assessment. A new administration proposal calls for this kind of review.

Defenders of these chemicals will no doubt provide the traditional responses: that studies using human subjects don't demonstrate a direct link between the chemicals and disease; that coincidence doesn't equal causality (although some coincidences strongly point to making a prudent instead of a reckless decision); and, the old standby, that tests on animals don't always, absolutely, inescapably translate to the same results in the human species. Each of these answers recalls the kind of reflexive response that Rachel Carson's work elicited from the chemical industry and the university scientists it subsidized. She anticipated the response, and wrote in *Silent Spring* of a public "fed little tranquilizing pills of half-truths. We urgently need an end to these false assurances, to the sugarcoating of unpalatable facts."

In the 1980s, especially when James Watt was at the Interior Department and Ann Gorsuch was at the EPA, the environmental know-nothings reached the peak of their influence. Poisoning the environment was almost regarded as a sign of hard-nosed economic pragmatism. In the Gorsuch EPA, for example, integrated pest management (IPM), the alternative to chemical pesticides, was literally declared anathema. The EPA banned publications about it, and certification of IPM methods was outlawed.

The Clinton-Gore administration began with a different view, and with a firm determination to turn the tide of pesticide pollution. Our policy pursued three imperatives: tougher standards, reduced use, and broader use of alternative biological agents.

Obviously, a sensible approach to pesticide use has to balance dangers and benefits and take economic factors into account. But we also have to take the heavy weight of special interests off the scale and out of the equation. The standards have to be clear and demanding, and the testing has to be thorough and honest. For too long we have set tolerance levels for pesticide residues in children hundreds of times higher than they should be. What calculus of economic benefits can justify this? We have to test the effects of these chemicals on children, not just adults, and we have to test a range of varying combinations. We must test not just to limit fear, but to limit what we have to fear.

If a pesticide isn't needed or doesn't work in a given situation, then the presumption should be against use, not for it. The benefit should be real, not possible, transitory, or speculative.

Above all, we have to focus on the biological agents for which the industry and its political apologists have such intense hostility. In *Silent Spring*, Carson wrote of the "truly extraordinary array of alternatives to the chemical control of insects." The array is wider today, despite the indifference of too many public officials and the resistance of manufacturers. Why don't we push hard for the use of nontoxic substances?

Finally, we must begin to bridge the cultural divide between the pesticide-production and agricultural community on the one side and the public health community on the other. People in the two communities come from different backgrounds, go to different colleges, and have very different viewpoints. As long as they face each other across a gulf of suspicion and enmity, we will find it hard to change a system in which production and profit are tied to pollution. One way in which we can signal the end of that system — and begin to narrow the cultural divide — is by having the Agricultural Extension Service promote alternatives to chemical solutions. Another is by instituting formal, ongoing dialogue between those who produce our food and those who protect our health.

The Clinton-Gore administration's new policy regarding pesticides had many architects. Maybe the most important was a woman whose last official government service came in 1952, when she resigned from her mid-level civil service position so she could write full-time, not just on weekends and at night. In spirit, Rachel Carson sits in on all the important environmental meetings of this administration. We may not do everything she would want, all at once, but we are moving in the direction she indicated.

In 1992, a panel of distinguished Americans selected *Silent Spring* as the most influential book of the last fifty years. Across those years and through all the policy debates, this book continues to be the voice of reason breaking in on complacency. It brought environmental issues to the attention not just of industry and government; it brought them to the public, and put our democracy itself on the side of saving the earth. More and more, consumer power will work against pesticide pollution, even when government does not. Reducing pesticides in food is now becoming a marketing tool as well as a moral imperative. The government must act, but the people can also decide — and I am convinced that the people will no longer let the government do nothing, or do the wrong thing.

Rachel Carson's influence reaches beyond the boundaries of her specific concerns in *Silent Spring*. She brought us back to a fundamental idea lost to an amazing degree in modern civilization: the interconnection of human beings and the natural environment. This book was a shaft of light that for the first time illuminated what is arguably the most important issue of our era. In *Silent Spring*'s final pages,

Carson described the choice before us in terms of Robert Frost's famous poem about the road "less traveled." Others have taken that road; few have taken the world along with them, as Carson did. Her work, the truth she brought to light, the science and research she inspired, stand not only as powerful arguments for limiting the use of pesticides but as powerful proof of the difference that one individual can make.

JOHN ELDER

Withered Sedge and Yellow Wood: Poetry in *Silent Spring*

RACHEL CARSON FRAMES *Silent Spring* with poetry. One of her two epigraphs comes from Keats's "La Belle Dame Sans Merci," while her concluding chapter, "The Other Road," takes its title from Frost's "The Road Not Taken." Such references are not surprising, given Carson's lifelong appreciation of literature. Even as a girl, she was a passionate reader and writer, publishing several of her early pieces in *St. Nicholas* magazine. During her first two years at Pennsylvania College for Women (subsequently renamed Chatham College) she was an English major; then she got to know the inspiring biology teacher Mary Scott Skinker and decided to devote herself to science instead. For the rest of her life, though, much of Carson's remarkable power as a writer came from her mastery of imagery, her apt allusions to literature, mythology, and history, and the cadenced, musical quality of her language. And great poetry remained her criterion for vivid, organic wholeness. In his book *House of Life*, Paul Brooks quotes Carson's remark upon receiving the National Book Award for her 1952 book *The Sea Around Us:* "If there is poetry in my book about the sea, it is not because I deliberately put it there, but because no one could write truthfully about the sea and leave out the poetry."

Carson's ability to transform our nation's environmental policies and practices through the writing of *Silent Spring* required the full array of her talents. She was simultaneously a gifted observer of nature, a scientist whose comprehensive perspective made her the most effective teacher of ecological principles for a worldwide audience, a woman of great courage who stood up to attacks from the chemical industry and its hired researchers, and a highly accomplished prose-stylist. I believe, however, that her references to Keats and Frost finally reflect more than Carson's general appreciation for literature and her talent for finding the apt quotation. They also ground her in a Romantic tradition of revolt against mechanical and hierarchical approaches to nature, and they convey the breadth of vision from which her prophetic power springs. Poetry, for Carson, was essential to the process of looking deeply into the world and making brave choices amid the clamor of competing opinions and interests.

Carson's decision to use lines from "La Belle Dame" as an epigraph came nearly at the end of her work on *Silent Spring*. She had been thinking of calling it something like

The War Against Nature, even though her agent, Marie Rodell, and her editor Paul Brooks were arguing for *Silent Spring*. In a final attempt to persuade Carson, Rodell showed her some lines from Keats that eloquently reinforced the latter of those two titles. As Linda Lear writes in her biography of Carson, "and so finally the book became *Silent Spring*." Specifically, Carson took for her epigraph the two lines with which Keats completed both the first and the final stanzas of his twelve-quatrain poem: "The sedge is wither'd from the lake, / And no birds sing." This turned out to be much more than an elegant complement to her new title. It anticipated the dramatic suspense within Carson's narrative, while also introducing her central connection between the health of the landscape and humanity's own well-being.

Keats's ballad begins in the voice of an unidentified speaker who meets a feverish, isolated man in a bleak landscape: "O what can ail thee, knight-at-arms, / alone and palely loitering?" From the fourth quatrain to the end of the poem, the knight gives his reply, telling the story of a fairy lover who first bewitched him and then left him alone to dream of "pale kings and princes . . . on the cold hill's side." A reader thus encounters the forlorn knight in his withered world first as a distressing mystery, which the poem subsequently explains with a tale of enchantment. In a parallel way, the blighting of the seasons that Carson observes all around her in 1950s America urgently calls for an explanation. Through her research into the poisonous chain of events that stills the songs of spring and threatens our own health, she uncovers yet another story of error and loss. The eighth chapter of *Silent Spring* makes a further direct reference to Keats in its title, "And No Birds Sing." And the opening sentences of that chapter read like Carson's extension of the ballad's imagery: "Over increasingly large areas of the United States, spring now comes unheralded by the return of birds, and the early mornings are strangely silent where once they were filled with the beauty of bird song. This sudden silencing of the song of birds, this obliteration of the color and beauty and interest they lend to our world have come about swiftly, insidiously, and unnoticed by those whose communities are as yet unaffected."

What can possibly account for such a nightmare of silencing and obliteration? In Carson's explanation, the careless use of chemical pesticides, not a demon lover, lies behind the hideous alterations of the world. She painstakingly explains the processes through which, after the landscape is blanketed with DDT from crop-dusters, toxicity spreads from the trees, fields, and streams to the insects, birds, and fish, and finally into the cells of our bodies. But if scientific explication replaces the ballad form in *Silent Spring*, that doesn't mean that Carson's is not in its own terms a tale of deathly enchantment. On the contrary, she views the heedless use of new chemical compounds in the decades following World War II as just one more form of enraptured folly. Just as the knight was seduced by his inhuman lover, Americans, in our consumerist frenzy, have given our hearts to a self-defeating dream of "the conquest of nature." Carson concludes her entire book with the sentence "It is our alarming misfortune that so primitive a science has armed itself with the most modern and terrible weapons, and that in turning them against the insects it has also turned them against the earth." We too learn the enormity of our error only upon awakening to the cold hillside of its consequences.

One of those expansive words that keeps getting away from us is *romantic*, which so often slips into conventional descriptions of love or, for that matter, gets applied dismissively to the naïve love of nature. (The word *ecological* teeters similarly on the edge of misappropriation — in danger of being identified with a set of social or political values to the exclusion of its specific scientific content.) But Carson's view of nature is in fact Romantic in ways that are specifically illuminated by English poetry at the end of the eighteenth and the beginning of the nineteenth centuries. The Romantic poets, including Keats and his grand predecessor Wordsworth, consciously opposed the overly analytical and categorizing tendencies of the Enlightenment. For them, an affirmation of nature's wholeness and humanity's participation in it was inevitably connected to revolt against the oppressiveness of urbanization, class privilege, and nationalistic warfare. As M. H. Abrams has written, "[t]hey set out, in various yet recognizably parallel ways, to reconstitute the grounds of hope and to announce the certainty, or at least the possibility, of a rebirth in which a renewed mankind will inhabit a renovated earth where he will find himself thoroughly at home."

Two points are especially salient in this comparison between Rachel Carson and the English Romantics. The first is that the poets, like Carson, refuted prevailing assumptions about the political order and rejected the claims of false authority. They thought of themselves, in Abrams's words, as "poet-prophets." Such angry rejection is also a prominent theme in *Silent Spring:* "Who has decided — who has the *right* to decide — for the countless legions of people who were not consulted that the supreme value is a world without insects, even though it be also a sterile world ungraced by the curving wing of a bird in flight? The decision is that of the authoritarian temporarily entrusted with power; he has made it during a moment of inattention by millions to whom beauty and the ordered world of nature still have a meaning that is deep and imperative." But even more fundamental to the Romantic worldview, and to Carson's, is hope. Those typically Romantic words in the passage quoted from Abrams — *reconstitute*, *rebirth*, *renewed*, and *renovated* — express confidence that humanity can return to a balanced and healthy way of living within the larger cycles of the earth. For Carson, "authoritarian" power is only temporary, because the people will awaken and demand to have restored to them what was lost "during a moment of inattention."

Carson is ultimately making a statement of *faith*, but not

one that is grounded in any sort of religious orthodoxy. Rather, it grows from her perception of beauty and health in the world as being at once immediate and transcendent facts. In a letter dated January 1, 1954, to her dear friend Dorothy Freeman, Carson quotes a passage from Keats's "Endymion" that begins "A thing of beauty is a joy forever: / Its loveliness increases; it will never / Pass into nothingness . . ." Such lines, for Carson as for Keats, are more than metaphorical; they express a direct, vital, and sustaining personal experience. Beauty endures mysteriously, even though the physical forms through which it passes may themselves vanish. And balance, even if sometimes overthrown, is always coming home within what Gary Snyder calls "the Main Flow" of the universe. Such a faith is nourished both by the revelations of literature and by the intricately interwoven physical world. In his book *Ecological Literary Criticism: Romantic Imagining and the Biology of Mind*, Karl Kroeber remarks that "Wordsworth's most significant 'nature poetry' is characterized by a conception of inclusive wholeness like that central to ecological thought." As the biologist leaves her highly controlled but sterile lab to move into the fertile messiness of ecological field work, she can say, with Wordsworth in "The Tables Turned," "Come forth into the light of things, / Let Nature be your teacher." Looking closely at the myriad lives and life cycles of the seashore — Carson's own special study — she can affirm with the closing of that poem, "Come forth, and bring with you a heart / That watches and receives."

Such a passionate revolt against worldviews that sever the vital connection between humanity and nature is never without allies. In one of the most heartbreaking of her letters to Freeman, written in March 1963, just a year before her death from cancer, Carson writes, "Oh — at long last, the first thin bubble of frog song came from the swamp Sunday night, after a warm, sunny day. And last evening I heard the first robin song. So spring is not to be silent!" As Wordsworth writes in the "Intimations" Ode, "Though much is taken, much remains." And much returns.

My wife, Rita, and I named our daughter Rachel, after Carson, out of gratitude for the difference she has made to our spring. By 1960, when *The New Yorker* began serializing *Silent Spring*, peregrine falcons and a number of other raptors had become extinct east of the Mississippi — unable to hatch their eggs because DDT in the environment had leached the calcium from the shells. But over the past several decades, as the pesticide's residues have become less and less prevalent, peregrines have been reintroduced to the part of Vermont where our family lives. With the help of ingenious tracking systems developed by the Peregrine Fund and Cornell University, these raptors have been established on south-facing cliffs like Deerleap, which juts out beside our own village of Bristol. At least one clutch of chicks is now fledged annually here, bringing these fastest of all aerial divers into the daily experience of their human neighbors. We can watch them circling about our homes and hear the *kek-kek-kek* of their calls. Sometimes we can even glimpse them blitzing down to the forest canopy below the cliffs, plummeting toward an unwary jay that has shown itself or a pigeon straying from a nearby barn. The presence of these raptors brings new beauty and drama to the seasons around our home. And they would not be here without the faith that motivated Carson, just as it did her Romantic ancestors.

To link Carson with the English Romantics does more than note a literary affinity. It associates her with an ongoing community of celebration and effort. She — like her predecessors and all those readers whom she has herself inspired — wants to take nature personally, to bring science and human values into a significant dialogue, and to resist callous or uninformed damage to the natural environment in the name of progress. Nature writers and explorers like John Muir, activists like David Brower, and contemporary authors like Gary Snyder and Terry Tempest Williams all participate in a broad effort to assert the integrity and sanctity of the living world against an irreverent program of technology and profiteering. For over two hundred years, the question has in effect been whether modern civilization, to which advanced science is so essential, can find a balanced view that is also respectful of what the writer David Abram calls "the more than human world." Poets remain crucial to this effort because their language acknowledges the full range of our human experience in images that become enduring opportunities for reflection and renovation. Anyone in our own day speaking out against the dredging of wetlands, the fragmentation of forests, or the deposition of carbon in the atmosphere that leads to global warming, in other words, has both the Romantics and Carson as ancestors and inspirations in a long but hopeful struggle.

In order to trace this lineage of sensitivity and commitment more specifically in Rachel Carson's own development, it is worthwhile to delve into her early reading. From a very young age, she was drawn to the stories of Beatrix Potter and to classic children's literature like *The Wind in the Willows.* Such anthropomorphized tales of animals were far from the scientific voice of her later studies. But, as Linda Lear has noted, they reinforced her perception of deep affinities between human beings and other forms of life. Another important influence on her thought was *St. Nicholas,* the outstanding magazine for children that Carson read devotedly while growing up. By publishing her own early writing in it, Carson joined a group of young contest-winners that included William Faulkner, F. Scott Fitzgerald, Eudora Welty, and E. B. White. Established poets, nature writers, and scientists were regularly published in the magazine as well, exemplifying how an emotional and aesthetic response to nature could be buttressed by a firm grasp of Darwinian principles. By connecting literature and science in its table of contents, the magazine sought to fulfill its mission of instilling in children "an ethical relationship with the natural world."

My wish to investigate the contents of *St. Nicholas* during the years when Rachel Carson was reading it led me to drive down to Hanover from Middlebury on a bright November morning. I wanted to check out the complete run of the magazine in the Dartmouth library. Belated flocks of Canada geese lifted and circled over the cornfields as I traveled south along the Connecticut River. Dartmouth's complete set of *St. Nicholas* was kept in the library's storage facility — a brown metal warehouse located on a dirt road far from the core of the campus. As the solitary patron of storage books on that Friday I worked my way through the volumes from 1912 to 1921 — increasingly amazed by the quality and range of this publication. Animal stories of all kinds were prominent, from the whimsical verses of the regular feature "For Very Little Folk" to ample selections from *Aesop's Fables* and the *Jataka Tales* to accounts of heroic dogs and of the individual lives and personalities of wild creatures. These narratives were generally emotional and personal, sometimes fantastic. But the pervasive tone was one of sympathy derived from imagining the vivid lives of our nonhuman neighbors. Such sympathetic imagination is vital to provoking what Carson was later to term "the sense of wonder."

It also naturally leads to a hunger for scientific knowledge about wild and domestic animals. One of the many excellent articles in the magazine's series on "Nature and Science for Young Folks" was "Birds as Travelers," published in December 1915 by Frank Chapman, who was the curator of ornithology at the American Museum of Natural History and whose field guides are still in use today. This discussion of migratory birds includes a superb explanation of different birds' "engines," with drawings of contrasting wing structures. But Chapman, too, was clearly interested in fueling sympathy, writing "And I shall be a poor historian if I do not arouse in you so strong an admiration for these skilful voyagers of the air that you will give them a hearty greeting when they come in the spring and wish them 'good luck' when they leave us in the fall."

A November 1920 item in the same "Nature and Science" series is titled "A Butterfly Mystery." Like Chapman's piece, this description of migrating monarch butterflies combines a scientific explanation of the life cycle of *Danaus plexippus* with awe at the sight of so many of the beautiful insects at rest in a grove of Monterey pines. (The trees, too, have their Linnaean name, *Pinus radiata*, included in the account.) Smeaton Chase, the author of this brief entry, first notes some "large clusters of dull-brown, dead leaves." But then, "as the clouds parted and the warm sunlight struck the tree I was gazing at, two or three leaves detached from a cluster and turned into large red butterflies." Knowledge and beauty are kindred experiences in this story. Such balance in the examples from *St. Nicholas* remains pertinent today as we ask how a deep, scientifically informed love of nature may still be cultivated in children. It's worth noting here that in Richard Louv's acclaimed book *Last Child in the Woods: Saving Our Children from Nature-Deficit Disorder* he not only cites Carson repeatedly but takes one of his own epigraphs from Walt Whitman ("There was a child went forth every day . . ."). Poetry, and the imaginative perspective it stimulates, retains the power both to encourage and to ratify close attention to the natural world.

One more feature from April 1917 is worth mentioning, with regard to *St. Nicholas*'s importance in transmitting Romantic insights and values to Rachel Carson as a girl. In that month's issue the "Heroes of To-day" feature focuses on "John Burroughs — The Seer of Woodchuck Lodge." In this biographical sketch of the most famous nature writer of his day, Mary Parkman both quotes from Emerson's poem "Each and All" and refers to Whitman. These writers were, with Thoreau, the most significant influences on Burroughs's own work, as well as being the conduits through whom Wordsworth and the English Romantics colored the American Renaissance. Burroughs was an excellent naturalist and a stern critic of "the naturefakers" of his day, with their sentimentalization of wild animals. But from Wordsworth he learned to interweave close observations of the seasons around his Catskill home with the self-disclosing voice of memoir. Immediately after her citation from Emerson, Parkman writes, "When John Burroughs writes about the birds, he brings with their life and song the feeling of the 'perfect whole' — the open fields, the winding river, the bending sky, and the cool fragrant woods. For he always gives, with the glimpses of nature that he culls, something of himself, something of his own clear-seeing, open-hearted appreciation." This description of Burroughs's voice anticipates so many of the lyrical naturalists who have inspired the American conservation movement from his time to the present, including Carson herself.

By concluding her book with a reference to "The Road Not Taken," Carson reinforces this sense of a continuing artistic movement with strong political and ecological implications. For Frost, as for Burroughs, Emerson and Thoreau represented the vital core of American tradition and served as conduits to the Wordsworthian fusion of landscape and autobiography. Like "La Belle Dame Sans Merci," "The Road Not Taken" was also far more significant to Carson's book than an isolated literary reference. When Frost died in 1963, a year before Carson and the year after *Silent Spring* was published, he was the best-known poet in America. Not only did he fuse close observations of nature with a highly personal and ironic voice, he was also an extraordinarily knowledgeable student of natural history, informed by his discerning awareness of Darwin and of the principles of evolution and ecology. A poem like "Spring Pools," from the 1928 volume *West-Running Brook*, reveals how skilled Frost was at exactly the sort of analysis Carson excelled in — tracing the influences on each organism of the annual water cycle. Unlike such predecessors as Wordsworth and Thoreau, however, Frost was rarely political in an overt sense. He always offered his intricate and suggestive poems, with their superb musicality, in the spirit of "a certain enigmatic reserve." A close reader of Frost's poems often falls *through* what initially seems their meaning, into an experience of irresolution. But such ambiguity strengthens the power of a poem like "The Road Not Taken," making it even more unlikely to leave a reader's mind as the seasons circle.

In framing her final chapter with this poem, Carson chose one of the best-known works of this celebrated figure. Its subtly varying five-line stanzas make it a delight to learn and say, and its final three verses give it a quotable moral: "Two roads diverged in a wood, and I — / I took the one less traveled by, / And that has made all the difference." The mischief in Frost is that these lines, like "Good fences make good neighbors," say, from "Mending Wall," seem at first reading to say more than the poem will finally allow. Further readings of "The Road Not Taken" amplify an essential ambivalence in the poem. It begins with a long delayed choice, as the speaker first gazes down one road "as far as I could," then, in the second stanza,

> . . . took the other, as just as fair,
> And having perhaps the better claim,
> Because it was grassy and wanted wear;
> Though as for that the passing there
> Had worn them really about the same.

"The Road Not Taken" expresses a sighing wistfulness about the unknowable meaning of our choices. When arriving at a branching road, we can never "travel both / And be one traveler." And "knowing how way leads on to way," we'll never really know what "all the difference" between our two potential paths has been. This uncertainty at the poem's heart doesn't it make it less powerful as a meditation on the importance of choices, though. To the contrary.

On August 31, 2006, a group of Vermonters set off on a five-day walk from central Vermont to Burlington, calling for governmental action on global warming. Our walk began at Bread Loaf, on a trail in the Green Mountain National Forest named for Robert Frost. My assigned role in the opening ceremony was to send us off with a reading of "The Road Not Taken." Our organizers' hope was to offer inspiration from a poet who had so often written about the landscape through which we would be walking. And the choice of reading seemed especially apt since we were asking for the United States to switch paths, from an economy and transportation system addicted to fossil fuels to one based on renewable sources of energy. I followed up the poem with the opening paragraph of Carson's final chapter, "The Other Road": "We stand now where two roads diverge. But unlike the roads in Robert Frost's familiar poem, they are not equally fair. The road we have long been traveling is deceptively easy, a smooth superhighway on which we progress with great speed, but at its end lies disaster. The other fork of the road — the one 'less traveled by' — offers our last, our only chance to reach a destination that assures the preservation of our earth."

An immediate appeal of bringing in Carson's reference was that she read the poem so well, both acknowledging its careful equivocation and building upon its eloquent focus on the importance of choice. Even more meaningful to us that morning at Bread Loaf, though, was the connection between Carson's opposition to the careless application of highly toxic substances in agriculture and the gravest environmental issue of our own time: pollution of the atmosphere by carbon that magnifies the greenhouse effect and alters the world's climate. Just as the reference to Keats did, Frost's poem gave Carson a way to connect the challenges of her own lifetime to a larger conversation about health and balance in the world. In the same way, Carson's achievement makes her, for us, a figure to conjure with as we confront the current global crises. She does not simply evoke the withered sedge, or return to the yellow wood, in a spirit of defeatism or confusion. Though she begins by focusing steadfastly on the worst, and explains the disastrous consequences of continuing in our errors, she also reminds us that "[t]he choice, after all, is ours to make." Her honesty, courage, and eloquence, like those of the poets she loved, remain a vital resource for lovers of the earth today.

JOHN HAY

A Long View of Rachel Carson

DURING THE COURSE OF my lifetime, I have seen people's attachments to their localities as quickly lost as they are found. The idea of permanence seems so easily discarded; one world is as carelessly dispatched as any other. It takes little to disengage ourselves from what we call "roots." In a country continually cutting itself away from its own land, I have often turned to the poetry of the earth and to those who could hear it and interpret its unending lessons. Without poetry, how could we reach the stars or know the seas? How could we survive the nihilism of a world that seldom consults what has been learned from history or from nature? I have seen two world wars in my life, and I now fear a third one may be on the horizon, if humanity continues to ignore its connections to nature. People who farm the land and fish the sea know that they must learn all the myriad details of their locality if they are to succeed in living with and from it. To know who you are, you need to know the earth and where you come from. Rachel Carson lived deeply in her localities and developed fierce attachments to the natural world in each of them. Her books made me feel at home on this planet in our era, when the human race has perpetrated the most lethal wars and inflicted the most massive damage upon nature in history.

After I was discharged from the army at the end of World War II — during which I barely escaped the deadly fate of so many friends — my wife, Kristi, and I left New York City and moved up to Cape Cod. For a few hundred dollars, I bought a plot of ten acres, "more or less," from an old Cape Codder who called it a "worthless woodlot." Our house was built on that tract while we lived in the house of my friend Conrad Aiken, the poet, when he and his wife, Mary, were away in England.

So began our life on the sandy shores of Cape Cod, a terminal moraine left behind by a continental ice sheet. Our house was perched on Dry Hill, looking out onto the northernmost shore of that sandy peninsula. I used to walk on as many beaches as I could, starting with the Great Beach along the exposed outer shores of the cape. As I watched the great rollers crashing at the head of the beach, I would wonder, where did they originate? What are waves, anyway? What is sand? Where did it come from? These questions were never raised when I was growing up.

After living for some time on Cape Cod, I was asked to join a group that was trying to get support for a Junior Museum that would hold classes with a connection to the outdoors. To put together a staff of volunteers, we tried to recruit people who had some knowledge of local details centered on the sandy shores. We were able to get scientists who knew something about what we now call "the environment," but each of them specialized only on one piece of the whole. Although at the time I did not yet have any special training in the natural sciences, I had grown up with a strong attachment to the wilderness, which I developed while summering in New Hampshire during vacations from New York City. On Cape Cod, I was asked to teach some classes at the Junior Museum. But what did I know about the sea and its shores? So I timidly started to learn about salt marsh grasses and invertebrates. I was well into my thirties, but I was beginning to see local horizons that I had never been conscious of before. These details of life were introducing me to a much wider range of interpretation than I had known up to then.

At the time, I was reading books such as *Our Plundered Planet* by Fairfield Osborn and *The Planet Eaters.* Like many other works after World War II, they declared that "Nature is dead." Such rhetoric bred a hopelessness, a sense of futility over trying to do anything to save it. Although these books woke me up to the horrors of what we were doing to the earth, they didn't give me much tangible substance that would help me understand the local horizon. It wasn't until I read Rachel Carson's books *The Sea Around Us* and *The Edge of the Sea* that I began to be conscious of the sea's wealth of details and the secrets it contained.

At first, I read Carson's books as if they were a kind of field guide, where I could find the immediate information I needed at the time. I had been led by our often mechanically guided world to think that any information might be available to me if I took the time to look it up. Guidebooks provide indispensable information, but they leave out something significant: what scientists do not know. It took me a long time to become aware that perhaps the sea I faced almost every day was not to be discovered from a field guide. The truth came from within and from the unknown.

Many works had already been written about the seashores, but these books didn't make me feel attached to them in any direct way; they looked only at the surface of things. Rachel Carson was the one who made me aware that, hidden in the tide pools, you could begin to reach the life of the great sea itself. She taught me that the tides and tidelands carry on the ancestral way of life on the planet. From her I began to realize that the shores of Cape Cod are made up of ancient grains of sand that hold the ageless secret of tenacity. Most of us are not so well-equipped as she was to realize that the sands are filled with tiny organisms carried in on the tidal waters. She understood that the real vastness of the planet can be understood only through infinitesimal detail.

When I first encountered Rachel Carson, I was only half-aware of the extent to which my life had been governed by the sea. Even though she spent time near us in Cape Cod and, later, on the coast of Maine, I never actually met her. I remember people talking about her and what she was writing. At the time, she was working at the Woods Hole biological research station, where she had a post with the U.S. Bureau of Fisheries. There she learned a great deal about carefully observing details in the field and studying how they fit together. I began to respect her from a distance. I then read her books, and they made all the difference. They opened up my eyes to a far more complex world than I'd ever been aware of before. I realized that I had to walk out to the edge of the sea to know it, to understand it.

Rachel Carson's vision was dedicated to what used to be called "Mother Earth," a term that's now out of fashion. She wrote about *connections* in nature. She had a gift for translating her ideas into an accessible language that caught the public's attention. With her talent for writing, she managed to find a way to weave together her scientific knowledge, her ease with poetic language, and her love of the sea. She was on solid ground when it came to Mother Earth; she knew it wasn't dying, in contrast to what so many other people were warning. She knew nature was still alive because she felt it in herself. Carson told us that Mother Earth would outlast us by millions of years. She also showed that we are all dependent on nature. She felt that, if people realized that, they would not be willing to blow everything up. It took quite a while for the public to realize the scope of what she was saying.

Rachel Carson wasn't just a scientist; she loved nature and was absolutely dedicated to it. She had enough self-training in science as well as in poetry to write about the mystery of life. She learned by picking things up and looking at them carefully. I had a feeling that, when she walked along the edge of the sea, she was going into the house of life. She wanted to put down everything she saw along the shores and to convey their mysteries to her readers with all the poetic skills she could muster. No other naturalist has matched her capacity to bring together such well-honed skills of observation, such a profound understanding of interconnections within the natural world, and such a transcendent writing style.

She realized that there are more organisms in the world than we can imagine. Life has its own magic, until people begin interpreting it in purely utilitarian terms. Some people love their own magic better than the real magic. Objectivity helps scientists to learn a lot, but not everything. Scientists don't want to talk about magic; they don't want to admit that man hasn't caused everything. But what we call magic is much more fascinating than what we give scientific labels to. Man is a visitor on this planet; we don't know how long his tenure will be. Some people walk along the beach and see a seashell, thinking it's empty, dead. But if you pick it up and put it to your ear, you can hear the sea and learn about where we come from.

Up in New Hampshire my family had a large garden at some distance from our house. My father had more than four hundred kinds of plants growing there. Insecticide use was pretty rudimentary back then. Only two kinds were used: something called Paris Green (whatever that was) and arsenic (which people also used to commit suicide). My mother would spray these insecticides against Japanese beetles that were attacking her roses. Anything that attacked her roses became her sworn enemy and had to be destroyed. Paris Green was not especially effective, so she used arsenic in the garden to get rid of not only Japanese beetles and other insects, but also rodents and the foxes that came after them, out of her general fear of the wilderness.

In those days, no one really knew what arsenic used as a garden insecticide might do to humans. The information was sprinkled all along the edges of things, so we never knew whether it applied to us. A local doctor who was a friend of the family got worried about the use of arsenic as an insecticide, so he went around collecting evidence on its possible effects as a poison. I remember him coming to our garden, testing a whole lot of things. He didn't accuse our family of anything, he just seemed concerned about the effects. At that age, I wasn't aware of what arsenic was. I just assumed that the things that adults did made sense, and one of those things was using Paris Green and arsenic to obliterate "pests." But, of course, these two insecticides were nothing compared to what came later.

DDT arrived in the 1950s, after I was married and living on Cape Cod. Everyone was very eager to use it, thinking it would be a panacea to "bugs" that bit or were otherwise bad. The authorities mounted public programs for spraying DDT to kill off gypsy moths and other insect pests. I recall a selectwoman who went around town on a pilgrimage pleading with people to spray DDT to "save our children." Somehow its use was linked to patriotism. The selectpersons were pretty primitive in their approach, employing theater at one point to promote the use of DDT.

People began spraying DDT on their properties, but they didn't know much about using it or what its effect might be. When word came that government planes were going to spray DDT in our area, we were told to pick up helium balloons from town hall to put on houses to warn planes not to spray over them. The helium drained out of the balloons I got, so I filled them with hot air and put them over our house. But the plane swooped over anyway, spraying everything. My wife, Kristi, remembers planes spraying the playground at the school where she taught.

The fiddler crabs were the first to suffer. The local people responsible for the salt marshes became aware that these crabs were dying in their burrows. They had a limited view of what the problem was; they didn't know what was causing the die-offs. Then frogs, fish, and other animals began dying, and some scientists began expressing concerns about DDT. I called off two government workers who came one day toting spray guns to apply the insecticide to the bog on our property below our house.

It took a long time for the public and for the authorities to realize that crabs, frogs, birds, people, and, in fact, the entire ecosystem were being affected by DDT. Biologists at Woods Hole had an understanding of the "ecosystem," but most ordinary people did not. To their credit, local people on Cape Cod were able to put an end to spraying the salt marshes. The authorities finally realized that the spraying programs were destroying what they were supposed to be protecting.

It was only later that I read Rachel Carson's brilliant work on DDT. It made me realize what was happening to life itself on the planet. When *Silent Spring* came out, it was viciously assailed by the petrochemical industry. Carson brought the full extent of the problems of DDT to the attention of the general public, and that was her crime, as far as representatives of the petrochemical industry were concerned. They found her book offensive because she was calling things by their real names, learning the actual facts about them. She was honest in every sense of the word. One company executive said the book's claims were preposterous, though he probably never read it. Other industry spokespeople thought she was attacking them personally and went after her by questioning her credentials and even her character. But she was a very gentle person and refused to ever sink as low as her detractors. Love motivated her work: love of nonhuman life, love of nature, love of the sea. Unless you love something, you're not going to stick with it, especially when standing up to people in power like those in the petrochemical industry. She just kept plugging away courageously at her research. But by then she was already quite sick with cancer. At times I wonder whether her death was hastened by stress brought on by the vitriolic assaults she had received after the publication of *Silent Spring.* The companies producing DDT never stopped attacking her, even after she died.

Silent Spring was written in the same voice as her other books, with the same breadth of vision and generosity of spirit. Everyone said, "Oh, this book is all about pesticides," but it wasn't merely that: it was an explanation of how things fit together in nature, how things *belong.* This was the same theme that ran throughout her writings: that life on this planet, in all its manifestations and depths, was something not manufactured by humankind. Someone who could see as much in nature as Rachel Carson did was really telling us about ourselves. What *Silent Spring* added to the conversation was what can happen when people act as though nature does not exist, as if Mother Earth were merely something sentimental. Carson traced the consequences of viewing ourselves as superior to all other creatures, of separating ourselves from nature. That isolation is what breeds aggression and wars. Carson's eye was a triumph over tragedy, but her warnings in *Silent Spring* went unheeded by those racing toward isolation from the rest of life.

Rachel Carson was a woman of great courage and tenacity. One characteristic that follows her life was her passion for the truth, no matter how far or deep she had to go to find it. If she could not find the truth from other people, she turned to nature to find it. She was never satisfied with the surface but explored the very depths of creation within the sea and its profound mysteries. She was not afraid to travel "Through caverns measureless to man / Down to a sunless sea," as Coleridge described it. Her writing passed over its underwater mountaintops and deep ravines, exploring the vast and nearly invisible sources of changes experienced by the manifestations of life on the surface.

Carson explored the great mysteries of life through a commitment that most of us could only dream about. She was never satisfied with surface explanations found in conventional guidebooks. These explanations were no substitute for work that probed deeply and inexhaustibly into the sea and its immense tides.

We assume that human beings are superior to all other species and that we have been assured a place at the top of the hierarchy. But it is the small things holding the world together. Rachel Carson understood this, paying attention to things as small as "the worlds in a grain of sand," as Blake put it. She used the sea as both a symbol and a focus of a world not beholden to humanity for its existence. She got attached to things in nature, even rocks and sand. Most people don't get attached to rocks and sand; they are afraid to. But anyone who reads or writes poetry will understand this. Her writing makes you feel so attached to nonhuman life that it can bring you to tears. With her ear for poetry, she listened to the sea and its often hidden worlds with profound attention. If we fail to listen, to wait, and to attach ourselves to this planet and its almost impenetrable variety, then we have turned ourselves into outsiders, ignorant of time, isolated from all forms of so-called nonhuman life whose roots have always been inseparable from our own existence. What can be the meaning of a land whose structure, root, and branch are being torn up and its integrity betrayed? The truth goes back a million years. What Rachel Carson's works should inspire in anyone in an age so threatened and brutalized by weapons of mass destruction is nothing less than her all-embracing love for nature, which was as deep and as powerful as the sea.

JANISSE RAY

Changing Sex

THERE WAS ONCE a town at the edge of America where plastics had been banned, as had all chemicals of dubious safety. Children ran around playing with wooden toys and leather balls, eating homemade cookies. The baker served steamed organic milk in earthenware mugs. People ate off pottery plates while sitting in wooden chairs at wooden tables.

In not one shop could an item of plastic be found. This meant that many things common in the modern world, including television, were nonexistent.

On the outskirts of town, alligators lounged on the banks of sloughs. A few hours of fishing delivered a mess of smallmouth bass. Between and beyond the farms, longleaf pines swayed and murmured in the hot subtropical summer.

In fall, along the rivers, cypress trees turned a shade of

wildflower honey and began to drop their needles in deep chocolate water. Red maples earned their name. In spring alligators bellowed their astonishing mating calls, and painted buntings, the most beautiful of migrants, could be glimpsed in the gnarled and moss-draped live oaks. Great blue herons and white ibis plundered the lake shallows.

The town had not always been this way. Once there had been plastic everywhere: bags, diapers, trash cans, bowls, spoons, bottles, toys. But the plastic kept breaking until the town dump was filled with it.

And the plastic didn't go away.

The people were a sensible lot. They had seen that plastics were not durable. Instead of a plastic wheelbarrow, why not repair grandpa's wooden one with the old iron wheel? The plastic flyswatter broke — better a metal handle sewn to a rectangle of leather. And so they passed a ban.

This town, of course, does not exist. But it could.

The first time I heard the term *endocrine disruption* was in 1994, the year Dr. Louis Guillette and his colleagues at the University of Florida released an important study. Guillette had begun investigating alligator health in 1985 to help alligator ranchers determine how many eggs they could collect from wild populations without harming them. What he discovered was that eggs were hard to find in Lake Apopka, near Orlando. Five years earlier, in 1980, a waste pond of Tower Chemical Company, located on Apopka's banks, overflowed, dumping the pesticides DDT and dicofol into the lake. After the spill, populations of juvenile alligators declined by 90 percent.

Exactly what was happening to the alligators?

Guillette stumbled upon a strange answer. He found that male alligators in Lake Apopka suffered testosterone levels three times lower than normal males found in Lake Woodruff, a similar but uncontaminated lake in a national wildlife refuge north of Orlando. In fact, male testosterone levels in Lake Apopka were close to those of females. Females, in turn, were "superfeminized," exhibiting twice the normal amount of estrogen.

With further studies, Guillette found that male alligators in Lake Apopka had poorly developed testes and phalli on average 24 percent smaller than those of Lake Woodruff males. Phalli were smallest near the Tower spill, now an EPA Superfund site. The Apopka females exhibited abnormal sexual organs as well. Follicles in their ovaries, instead of housing one egg, might house up to four.

When Guillette repeated his studies in the lab, painting half of the "clean" eggs collected from Lake Woodruff with contaminants, the results replicated those from the field.

Testosterone is necessary for penile growth, and Guillette noticed a positive relationship between testosterone levels in the blood and penis size in Lake Woodruff alligators. But this did not hold true in Lake Apopka. An Apopka alligator's penis size was not indicative of the amount of testosterone in its blood. Guillette realized that chemicals were disrupting animals' reception of their own hormones.

Silent Spring opened the floodgates of inquiry into environmental contaminants and their effects on wildlife and humans, an investigation that accelerated in the 1990s. We've looked at chemicals in high doses as lethal. We've looked at chemicals as carcinogenic. But they may be affecting us in other life-threatening ways.

In the past two decades, study after study has shown what Rachel Carson predicated. Chemicals are disturbing normal hormone-controlled development, affecting gender, sex, and reproduction. And, we are now seeing, low doses are disruption enough.

Fish appear particularly at risk of hormone disruption. Near a bleached kraft paper mill on Lake Superior, white suckers exhibited lower levels of hormones, took longer to mature, developed smaller sexual organs, and, once mature, produced fewer eggs. Some eggs refused to grow, although some did hatch, and some of these larvae survived. Lake whitefish showed similar results.

Four miles downstream from pulp and paper mills in north Florida's Fenholloway River, mosquitofish females developed a male sex organ called a gonopodium and attempted to mate with female fish. The scientific term for dual sex anatomy is *intersex*, which means an abnormal presence of traits of both sexes in one specimen. Intersex roach, as well as other species of fish, were found in rivers in the United Kingdom, with incidences significantly higher downstream of sewage treatment works.

Recently, the fish pathologist Vicki Blazer, searching for a reason for a die-off of smallmouth bass in the South Branch of the Potomac River, found that almost all the male bass surveyed were intersex in that they contained immature eggs in their testes. They also had lower sperm counts and the sperm were less motile than in healthy bass.

The abnormalities, of course, are not restricted to fish.

Scientists have found female marine snails that developed male genitalia. They've found gulls becoming feminized, meaning a sex ratio skewed toward the female, with many males not mating or parenting. One beluga whale in the St. Lawrence estuary of Quebec had two ovaries, two testes, male genitalia, and partial female organs. Female black bears in Alberta have exhibited some degree of male sex organs.

In fact, a report published in 2003 by the Scientific Committee on Problems of the Environment and the International Union of Pure and Applied Chemistry states that more than two hundred animal species are known or suspected to have reproductive disorders that might be attributed to endocrine disrupting chemicals (EDCs), synthetic compounds that, when absorbed in the body, disrupt its natural functions. Over 100,000 chemicals, most inadequately tested, are now on the market.

Our endocrine system is composed of glands — including the hypothalamus, pineal, pituitary, thyroid, thymus, adrenal, kidney, pancreas, ovaries, and testes — that secrete hormones. These hormones, including adrenaline, insulin, thyroxin, estrogen, testosterone, androgen, and melatonin, are secreted directly into the bloodstream. Since hormones function away from their source (the pituitary serves as the control center) they are known as messengers. The human endocrine system controls growth, metabolism, and fertility, and assists our bodies in tasks both minor and major, such as reaction to fear, transformation during puberty, control of brain development, and storage of energy.

A developing fetus receives messages not only through its own hormone system but also its mother's. These signals guide its development, shaping characteristics as blatant as number of toes to those as intricate as details of the brain.

Some chemicals are more proven than others to cause endocrine disruption.

DDT, of course, bioaccumulated in wildlife and caused eggshell thinning, leading to reduced populations of many bird species.

Diethylstilbestrol, or DES, is a synthetic estrogen that was prescribed to millions of pregnant women in the United States from the 1940s to the 1970s to prevent miscarriage. It causes a rare form of vaginal cancer in daughters of women who took the hormones and other adverse affects in both daughters and sons.

For fifty years polychlorinated biphenyls (PCBs) were used in products ranging from fluorescent light fixtures to adhesives to coolants inside electronics. Though they were banned in the United States in 1977 and are restricted through much of the world, PCBs remain in the environment and can be found in our food chain, including in mothers' milk.

Many, many other pesticides and chemicals are suspected to be EDCs.

I love macro, not micro. I'm not a chemist. I don't want to be writing about chemicals, undetectable by the raw senses and invisible. At least Rachel Carson could see the white powder of DDT falling from airplanes and dusting the world. I want to write about the polar bear swimming with her cub, looking for solid ice as the climate changes. About caribou running like a low dark cloud across the Arctic plain in advance of the oil drillers. About trees whispering west to east, until the message arrives to the most remote tree in the most remote wilderness that Judge Elizabeth LaPorte of the U.S. District Court of California has upheld the Roadless Initiative. I want to write about the oldest mountains in the world, lined up, their tops waiting to be blasted away. Visible dangers.

When Guillette's initial studies were published, I was a graduate student at the University of Montana, a hotbed of environmental advocacy. Almost immediately the Clark Fork Coalition, a Missoula watershed group, tackled dioxins and began a campaign to reduce demand for chlorine-whitened products. Dioxin is a generic term that refers to a group of chemicals formed during industrial processes like bleaching. Known to be carcinogenic, dioxins were made infamous by Lois Gibbs of Love Canal.

The university campaign worked. Campuswide, if you used a copier, your copies slid out on light gray paper.

I was an easy convert. Not long after becoming an adult, I had learned that white rice was bleached, as was white sugar, as was white flour, and I happily switched to brown, turbinado, and whole wheat. For this I thank the hippies, whose ranks I joined in the 1980s. A rush toward white reversed, and bark-leaf-dirt brown became a holy color. Who wanted to be ingesting bleach? Yet we were, hourly.

That's when I first thought about sanitary napkins and tampons, hiding in their pure whiteness chemicals worn for long hours next to mucous membranes. Along with thousands of other women, I turned to unbleached sanitary products or rewashable cloth pads.

Suddenly, at least in the households I knew, dioxin was a familiar word. The world seemed, there in Missoula, that it might turn away from bleach entirely.

I am walking along the edge of the ocean on Cape Cod as the tide goes out, beachcombing. The strand is a long line of seaweed, tangled around sand dollars, whelk shells, and a rare New England neptune. I am an inveterate scavenger. I love digging old middens and dumps for decorated pottery shards, antique bottles, and rusted car parts. But the newer dumps I hate, for they cause me embarrassment for my culture. There is so much plastic, which breaks and breaks yet never vanishes. Which doesn't last, yet does. Now the seaweed is full of plastic — quart oil bottle, surgi-

cal glove, broken Styrofoam. I am picking up pink tampon applicators. In protest, I am going to send them back to the company from where they came.

This summer my husband and I joined a Vermont initiative to get as many people as possible consuming only local foods for a week. The object was to support a local food system and to understand what might happen to the food supply if fossil fuels became scarce. About one hundred fifty people signed up for the initiative, bravely vowing to forego coffee and bananas and chocolate. That might have been a long week, except that every night a different household sponsored a potluck. Midweek, my husband and I followed directions to a home outside town, the apartment of a couple we didn't know, Tracy and C.B.

Tracy is a woman in her late twenties, with strawberry blond hair. When we arrived she was standing at the stove making bean patties, wearing a long skirt. We introduced ourselves and offered the salad we brought — all the vegetables were from our garden. The apartment was orderly, with a cat post and a Diego Rivera print.

"C.B. will be back soon," Tracy said. "He's gone to pick someone up."

Soon C.B. entered with one other dinner guest. C.B. is Tracy's husband, but we were at first confused because he looked like a woman, with a feminine figure and delicate features. He wore jeans and a plain T-shirt, his dark hair cropped short.

One of the first things Tracy did was offer us water. We

had brought plastic water bottles, but she wrinkled her nose and made her filtered, deep-well water served in a glass sound so delicious that we accepted. Tracy is an environmental studies graduate student, we found out, a person deeply concerned about toxins in the environment.

She explained that hazardous chemicals are found in plastic, possibly even in Nalgene. "C.B. and I use stainless steel water bottles," she said, opening the cabinet to exhibit them.

The five of us took plates, served ourselves, and settled down to eat. "What are you studying?" I asked Tracy.

The question had no simple answer. For me to understand her thesis, she had to start at the beginning. Tracy began to talk about toxins and endocrine disruption. She spoke brilliantly, quickly. Any question I asked she could answer. She cited studies, explained difficult chemical processes. She rattled off chemical compounds as if they were old enemies.

We were hardly eating. We were talking. Tracy, flooded with passion about toxicology, ran upstairs for current issues of *Environmental Health Perspectives* and for a copy of *Our Stolen Future*, the 1996 book by Theo Colborn, Dianne Dumanoski, and John Peterson Myers that first called attention to the interference of hormonal messages by synthetic chemicals. How had I missed this book?

"We've made our kitchen nearly plastic-free," she said proudly, and leapt up again to show us test tubes that held spices, Mason jars for leftovers.

For the entire meal, this was our conversation: *phthalates* and *bisphenol A* and *estradiol. Phenotypes* and *mutagenesis*. It was a vocabulary entirely new to me. My head was swimming.

As Tracy spoke I jotted down a few sources, and before we left I asked if I could meet with her again.

Some EDCs are environmental estrogens, which do harm by mimicking estradiol, the principal and most potent estrogen (produced by the developing follicle cells) in the ovary, and by binding to estrogen receptors. These EDCs include the pesticide methoxychlor; certain PCBs; bisphenol A (BPA), used to manufacture baby bottles, water bottles, and dental sealant; DES; and phytoestrogens, meaning plant-based estrogens, found particularly in soybeans. Other chemicals, however, are antiestrogens, meaning that they combat the reception of estrogen: the fungicide vinclozolin; pp'DDE, a metabolite of DDT; and certain PCBs and phthalates.

Problems are showing up not only in the reproductive health of those who have been exposed, and not only in the development of their offspring, but in the reproductive health of their offspring.

For a decade Frederick vom Saal of the University of Missouri has been looking at BPA. He has established that male offspring of female mice exposed to BPA have enlarged prostates, smaller testes, decreased sperm counts, malformed sperm, and decreased sperm motility. Female offspring exhibit, among other traits, early-onset puberty, deformed vaginal structures, polycystic ovaries, and increased numbers of miscarriages.

Earl Gray, a toxicologist for the Environmental Protection Agency, found that the male offspring of rats exposed to vinclozolin were born with nipples, malformed scrota and testes, and vaginal pouches. Some of them had phalli with hypospadias, which are urethral openings found not at the penis tip but along its shaft or in the scrotum. This latter finding is particularly sobering given that the rate of hypospadias in human babies doubled inexplicably between 1968 and 1993.

Phthalates (pronounced *thal-ates*) are chemicals used in solvents, in soft plastics (like shower curtains and baby toys), and in plastic packaging. For example, DEHP — di(2-ethylhexyl) phthalate — is the main plasticizer in polyvinyl chloride. DBP — dubutyl phthalate — is common in personal care products such as lotions, fragrances, cosmetics, and deodorants, as well as in pharmaceutical coatings. Most people carry a body burden of phthalates.

Shanna Swan, a professor and researcher at the University of Rochester, analyzed urine samples of pregnant women for phthalates and later examined the male infant offspring of those women. She found that "prenatal phthalate exposure at environmental levels can adversely affect male reproductive development in humans." High levels of phthalates (albeit levels below those assumed to be safe by the EPA) correlated with reduced scrotal size, smaller penises, and interrupted testicular descent. But the most astounding breakthrough was a correlation between phthalates and reduced anogenital distance, or distance between the anus and the base of the penis. The anogenital index (AGI) is important as a marker in endocrine research, since it predicts the healthy development of genitals.

Apparently, phthalate exposure in utero reduces testosterone production, which can result in malformations and incomplete development of the genitalia in boys. In fact, a mother exposed to DBP was ten times more likely than an unexposed mother to birth a child with a short AGI.

This has become known as phthalate syndrome.

Phthalates have been linked to other reproductive system problems.

In the early 1990s, doctors in Puerto Rico noticed a distressing trend — early-onset puberty. Precocious puberty is defined as secondary sex characteristics occurring before age eight in girls (menarche before age nine) and before age nine in boys. In Puerto Rico, girls as young as six months old showed premature thelarche, or breast development.

In blood samples taken from the thelarche patients, 68 percent indicated high levels of phthalate esters, including DEP, DBP, and DEHP. The cause(s) of this spike in premature puberty are unknown, but speculations include soy formula, the mouthing of plastic toys and pacifiers, and food and water that has been in contact with plastic wrapping and food containers. (Puerto Rico, being an island, imports much of its food.)

Other studies have found precocious puberty caused by

haircare products that contain hormone additives. The traits have been known to subside once use of the products discontinues.

In 1996 researchers Joseph and Sandra Jacobson published a study documenting a possible link between PCBs and human intelligence. Mothers with the lowest concentrations of PCBs in their blood birthed children with higher IQs than mothers with the highest concentrations. The children with less exposure also had better memory and attention.

Let's look at other problems in human sexuality. Could endocrine-disrupting chemicals be linked to infertility? Difficulties with conception are so ubiquitous that a new magazine called *Conceive* has been founded. I know many couples who have been able to conceive only via medical intervention, sometimes radical, and who call their babies miracles. Other friends have never been able to bear children.

Sex ratios, or the number of female to male births, have been reported skewed in some places. The Aamjiwnaang First Nation community of Ottawa has experienced a severe decline in boys born in the five years before 2005. The Aamjiwnaang live near several large chemical and petrochemical plants.

The possible consequences of chemicals on humans are deeply disturbing. Infertility. Distorted sex ratios. Lowered sperm quality. Lowered sperm motility. Precocious puberty. Undescended testes. Genital malformations. Intersex infants.

I am hiking in Nova Scotia, along the Bay of Fundy, where the tides are forty-five to fifty-four feet high. In the flotsam and jetsam, along with the starfish and egg cases of skates, I find pink plastic tampon applicators. I pick them up to mail back.

During the evening we spent with Tracy and C.B., I finally got up my nerve to ask Tracy a question, something I'd been thinking about. I warned her that the question might sound strange, and that I wouldn't be offended if she didn't answer. It was something I'd been thinking about.

A little background is important here. My husband and I have a dear friend, a young woman we watched grow up, whom I'll call Anna. I met Anna when she was eight, in school with my son. We're friends of her family; in fact, they're like family. We've vacationed together, spent holidays together.

A few years ago, while backpacking for five days in Montana wilderness, my conversation with Anna briefly turned to sexuality. She said she identified with being transgender, a term I didn't understand then. I asked her to explain, but even after she attempted, still I didn't understand. I was thinking she meant androgynous, since Anna attempted to look neither male nor female, but kept her hair short, wore baggy clothing, never wore skirts or makeup, and never carried a purse.

Anna went off to college and we didn't see her so often. This past summer we happened to be in New York City, where Anna is living, and we arranged to meet her for an afternoon at the Met. We were sitting on the big white steps in hot summer sunshine when Anna told us that she had always felt like a boy, that she was going to change her sex, that she was in New York for hormone therapy.

"Would you mind calling me Andrew?" she asked.

Tears sprang to my eyes. I hugged her, now him. "Of course," I said. "From now on you are Andrew to us."

This is not a story about being transgender. That subject is too personal, too political, too nuanced. On occasion I had met transgender people. But at Tracy and C.B.'s home, for the second time in a month, I was sitting with a transgender person. Suddenly I was calling a friend who looked like a she a he. He, him, his. I was watching my young friend Anna/Andrew using the men's bathroom, and listening to him tell me about not being able to check either gender box on job applications.

Recently I had been hearing more about gender variance, and sometimes gender ambiguity. In a gallery I had seen a photograph of a young man with scars where breasts had been, lying beneath his young male lover. Another male-turned-female transgender person I knew was dating a female-turned-male transgender person.

"Do you think there is an upswing in numbers of transgender people?" I asked Tracy. "Could issues of gender variance or gender ambiguity have anything to do with environmental toxins and endocrine disruption?"

Honestly, I expected Tracy to be shocked and to scorn such a politically incorrect question. But she brightened even more and jiggled excitedly in her chair.

"Yes, yes!" she said. "I think so."

I glanced at C.B., who we by now knew to be transgender. He was nodding. "Is there any work in this area?"

"Work, yes," Tracy said. "But few studies published yet. People have been studying animals and not attempting many hypotheses about human changes and EDCs. Yet."

Yet. But if fish can switch sexes, or exhibit traits of both genders, why not humans? If exposure to endocrine-disrupting chemicals causes sexual variance in animals, why not in humans?

"What if C.B. was biologically a boy at conception, but chemicals in utero changed his development?" Tracy asked. "I don't think that being intersex or being trans is a problem, any more than being just male or just female is a birth defect. But when we start having babies who are developing in one direction and switch them chemically to develop differently, it shows that chemicals are powerful and are affecting us at levels many of us are exposed to on a daily basis."

"This is a sign to start paying more attention," she said.

In October 2005, *Environmental Health Perspectives* published an article asking the million-dollar question: might prenatal and childhood exposure to EDCs be responsible for a variety of abnormalities of human sexuality, gender development and behaviors, and reproductive capabilities? Christine Johnson, on Trans-health.com, the online magazine of health for transsexual and transgender people, said that an "increasing amount of evidence" links the proliferation of EDCs to "variations in gender identity and sexual orientation."

I am strolling along Bimini's beach. The strand is littered with trash, which gets dumped in the ocean, much of it plastic. I am walking the Oregon coast, finding discarded fishing line and empty bags. I am hiking one of the wildest beaches on the Atlantic coast, Cumberland Island, part of which is a wilderness area. Washed up on the beach I am finding medical syringes, a flip-flop, plastic rope, a crab float, faded pink tampon holders.

But not only reproductive and gender-related systems are affected. The endocrine system regulates all hormone activity; the negative effects may be legion. Declining intelligence. Immune suppression. Behavioral abnormalities. Sleep abnormalities. Testicular cancer. Prostate cancer. Breast cancer. Hyperthyroidism. Obesity. Diabetes.

All over the world, citizen-advocacy groups are calling for decreased exposure to chemicals. Women's Voices for the Earth, based in Missoula, Montana, is pushing for nail polishes containing the phthalate DBB to be pulled from the market. The Pesticide Action Network is working to ban the use of lindane in shampoos and lotions. Campaign Whale wants to bring attention to the effects of EDCs on already beleaguered whales. The Chemical Injury Information Network publishes a monthly magazine, *Our Toxic Times*. Health experts and scientists are protesting the

World Health Organization's recent call to renew the use of DDT to fight malaria in African countries.

Stephen Safe of the Department of Veterinary Physiology and Pharmacology at Texas A&M University opposes the EDC theory, one of few academic scientists who do. "The role of endocrine disrupters and human disease has not been fully resolved," he writes. "However, at present the evidence is not compelling." He cites studies that indicate no changes in sperm counts over time and suggests that diet may be the cause of many hormone-related problems. Safe reminds us that life expectancy in this country has doubled. "It is [also] important to carefully validate and replicate findings before media announcements that may contribute to unnecessary fear and worry by the public," he says.

His stance resembles that of the American Chemical Council. The chemical industry has funded numerous studies that conclude that endocrine disruption is not harmful.

But evidence mounts, study after chilling study, until I am convinced that worldwide exposure to endocrine-disrupting chemicals is a dangerous, unplanned, vast experiment in human health, the upshot of which we may not realize for generations to come.

My family has rallied to weaken the role of plastic in our household, and to avoid pesticides, herbicides, and chemicals in general. We've mostly replaced bleach with peroxide and we buy unbleached products. We clean with baking soda and vinegar. We've bought stainless steel water bottles.

We need to scour another level deeper.

I suggest an initiative to do without plastics for a week, as we did without imported food, and immediately I begin to wonder how I can ever, even with my cloth grocery bags and pottery lids, do without. Plastic is everywhere. A plastic bag is so useful.

But I don't want a throwaway legacy. If someone someday combs across the beaches of my spent life, I want him or her to find, washed up there, whole and story-laden artifacts, not toxic but indicative, along with shards of courage and truth. While all around the beachcomber, life goes on.

TERRY TEMPEST WILLIAMS

The Moral Courage of Rachel Carson

RACHEL CARSON has never been more relevant. And yet more than forty years after the publication of *Silent Spring*, we still do not seem to have fully absorbed her message of caution and prudence regarding the power of pesticides. We are still walking down the path of environmental degradation. The parable that opens the door to *Silent Spring* appears even less fictional now:

> There was once a town in the heart of America where all life seemed to live in harmony with its surroundings . . . Then a strange blight crept over the area and everything began to change. Some evil spell had settled on the community: mysterious maladies swept the flocks of chickens; the cattle and sheep sickened and died. Everywhere was a shadow of death. The farmers spoke of much illness

> among their families . . . There was a strange stillness. The birds, for example — where had they gone? . . . It was a spring without voices . . . No witchcraft, no enemy action had silenced the rebirth of new life in this stricken world. The people had done it themselves.

Rachel Carson. I first heard her name from my grandmother. I must have been seven or eight years old. We were feeding the birds — song sparrows, goldfinches, and towhees — in my grandparents' yard in Salt Lake City, Utah.

"Imagine a world without birds," my grandmother said as she scattered seed and filled the feeders. "Imagine waking up to no birdsong."

I couldn't.

"Rachel Carson," I remember her saying.

Later, at the breakfast table, she and my grandfather engaged in an intense discussion of the book they were reading, *Silent Spring*, as my mind tried to grasp what my grandmother had just said about a muted world.

Decades later, I found myself in a used bookstore in Salt Lake City. The green spine of *Silent Spring* caught my eye. I pulled the classic off the shelf and opened it. First edition, 1962. As I reread various passages, I was struck by how little had changed. Each page was still a shock and a revelation.

> One of the most tragic examples of our unthinking bludgeoning of the landscape is to be seen in the sagebrush lands of the West, where a vast campaign is on to destroy the sage and to substitute grasslands. If ever an enterprise

> needed to be illuminated with a sense of the history and meaning of the landscape, it is this. For here the natural landscape is eloquent of the interplay of forces that have created it. It is spread before us like the pages of an open book in which we can read why the land is what it is, and why we should preserve its integrity. But the pages lie unread.

The pages still lie unread.

Rachel Carson is a hero of mine. She remains a regal and revolutionary figure within the conservation community, a towering example within American democracy of how one person's voice can make an extraordinary difference both in public policy and in the minds of the populace. Her name and her vision of a world intact and interrelated have entered mainstream culture.

Even so, I wonder how many of us have ever really read *Silent Spring*? We can all rattle off a two-sentence summation of its text: "All life is connected. Pesticides enter the food chain and not only threaten but destroy it." And yet I fear that its status as "an American classic" allows us to nod to its power but to miss the subtleties and richness of the book as both a scientific treatise and a piece of distinguished literary nonfiction.

Rachel Carson presents her discoveries of destruction in the form of storytelling. In example after example, grounded in the natural world, she weaves together facts and fictions into an environmental tale of life, love, and loss. Her voice is graceful and dignified, but sentence by sentence she delivers right-hand blows and counterpunches to the status quo ruled by chemical companies within the kingdom of agriculture.

> If the Bill of Rights contains no guarantee that a citizen shall be secure against lethal poisons distributed either by private individuals or by public officials, it is surely only because our forefathers, despite their considerable wisdom and foresight, could conceive of no such problem.

The facts she presents create the case against "biocide." We are killing the very fabric of nature in our attempt to rid the world of pests through these "elixirs of death." She indicts the insecticides by name: DDT, chlordane, heptachlor, dieldrin, aldrin, and endrin. And then adds to the toxic hydrocarbons the alkyl or organic phosphates, among the most poisonous chemicals in the world: parathion and malathion.

The fictions she exposes are the myths we have chosen to adopt in our obsession to control nature. She reminds us of the story of Medea, the Greek sorceress who became overwrought with jealousy because of her husband's love of another woman. Medea presents the new bride with a gift, a robe that will immediately kill whoever wears it. It becomes a garment of death. Carson calls our use of pesticides "death by indirection." We are killing insects and in turn killing ourselves, as these toxins slowly and violently enter the waters and eventually our own bloodstreams.

Rachel Carson did not turn her back on the ongoing chronicle of the natural history of the dead. She chose to bear witness. "It is time," she said, "that human beings admit their kinship with other forms of life." If we cannot accept this moral ethic, then we are complicit in the killing. With each chapter she adds to our understanding of the horrors of herbicides and hydrocarbons, the web of life unraveling. It is impossible for the reader not to be mindful of Carson's emotional and intellectual stamina, her ability to endure the pain of the story she was telling.

But Carson had a vision. "Sometimes I lose sight of my goal," she wrote in an essay in her first year of college. "Then again it flashes into view, filling me with a new determination to keep the vision before my eyes."

Hers was a conscientious and directed soul. She believed in the eloquence of facts. She loved both language and landscape. "I can remember no time when I wasn't interested in the out-of-doors and the whole world of nature," Carson said.

Writing became the expression for her passion toward nature. She published her first story when she was ten years old, winning the Silver Badge from the prestigious children's magazine *St. Nicholas.* "Perhaps the early experience of seeing my work in print played its part in fostering my childhood dream of becoming a writer," she later said.

Here was a young woman already on her path. In 1929 she graduated magna cum laude from Pennsylvania College for Women, now Chatham College, with a major in zoology. The strength of her coursework in both science and literature provides evidence of her dual nature as a scientist and a poet. "I thought I had to be one or the other," she said. "It never occurred to me that I could combine two careers."

Carson's editor and biographer, Paul Brooks, wrote that "the merging of these two powerful currents — the imagination and insight of a creative writer with a scientist's passion for the fact — goes far to explain the blend of beauty and authority that was to make her books unique."

Perhaps this is Rachel Carson's gift to us: seeing the world whole.

Carson continued her education as a biologist, receiving a master's degree in zoology at Johns Hopkins University, where she studied genetics. Her thesis, "The Development of the Pronephros During the Embryonic and Early Larval Life of the Catfish (*Ictalurus punctatus*)," should quell the ongoing criticism that she was merely an "amateur naturalist."

In 1936 she accepted a position with the United States Bureau of Fisheries, which later became the U.S. Fish and Wildlife Service, as an aquatic biologist. Here she was able gracefully to fuse her talents as a scientist and a writer, eventually becoming chief of publications for the bureau. Early in her tenure at Fish and Wildlife, she also taught courses at the University of Maryland and at Johns Hopkins.

Under the Sea-Wind was published in 1941. *The Sea Around Us* was published in 1951, to great popular and critical acclaim, and received the National Book Award in nonfiction. It remained on the *New York Times* bestseller list for months. "If there is poetry in my book about the sea," she said, "it is not because I deliberately put it there, but because no one could truthfully write about the sea and leave out the poetry."

In 1955, four years after the success of *The Sea Around Us*, Carson published *The Edge of the Sea*, extending her readers' knowledge of the ocean to the ocean's interface with the land. She brought her naturalist's eye to the intricacies of tide pools and illuminated the habitats of the sandy beach and the rocky shore.

And then came *Silent Spring*.

Rachel Carson received a burning letter from her friend Olga Owens Huckins, a journalist, who asked for help in finding people who could elucidate and speak to the dangers of pesticides. The Huckinses had a small place in Duxbury, Massachusetts, just north of Cape Cod, which they had made into a bird sanctuary. Without any thought of the effects on birds and wildlife, the state had sprayed the entire area for mosquito control.

Huckins sent a letter of outrage to the *Boston Herald* in January 1958. Here is an excerpt:

> The mosquito control plane flew over our small town last summer. Since we live close to the marshes, we were treated to several lethal doses as the pilot crisscrossed our place. And we consider the spraying of active poison over private land to be a serious aerial intrusion.
>
> The "harmless" shower bath killed seven of our lovely songbirds outright. We picked up three dead bodies the next morning right by the door. They were birds that had lived next to us, trusted us, and built their nests in our

> trees year after year. The next day three were scattered around the birdbath. (I had emptied it after the spraying but YOU CAN NEVER KILL DDT.) . . .
>
> All of these birds died horribly and in the same way. Their bills were gaping open, and their splayed claws were drawn up to their breasts in agony.

Olga Owens Huckins bore witness. Rachel Carson responded. Four and a half years later, *Silent Spring* was published. Carson wrote to Huckins that her letter had "started it all" and had led Carson to realize that "I must write the book."

This was a correspondence between friends, two women, individuals standing their ground in the places they loved, each engaging the gifts she possessed to make a difference in the world. We can never forget the power of impassioned, informed voices sharing their stories of place, bearing witness, speaking out on behalf of the land they call home.

Rachel Carson told the truth as she saw it. The natural world was dying, poisoned by the hands of power tied to corporate greed. Her words became a catalyst for change. She made a striking parallel between nuclear fallout and the fallout from pesticides:

> Along with the possibility of the extinction of mankind by nuclear war, the central problem of our age had therefore become the contamination of man's total environment with such substances of incredible potential for harm — substances that accumulate in the tissues of plants and animals and even penetrate the germ cells to shatter or alter

the very material of heredity upon which the shape of the future depends.

A debate had begun: a reverence for life versus a reverence for industry. Through the strength and vitality of her voice, Carson altered the political landscape of America.

Loren Eisely wrote that *Silent Spring* "is a devastating, heavily documented, relentless attack upon human carelessness, greed, and responsibility." Not everyone saw it that way. The Monsanto Chemical Company, anticipating the publication of the book, urgently commissioned a parody entitled "The Desolate Year" to counteract Carson's attack on the industry. Its intent was to show the pestilence and famine that the company claimed would occur in a world without pesticides.

Robert White-Stevens, a biochemist who was the assistant director of the Agricultural Research Division of American Cyanamid, became the chemical industry's chief spokesman. He made more than twenty-eight speeches against *Silent Spring.* He was particularly upset by the evidence against DDT, charging that Carson was "a fanatic defender of the cult of the balance of nature."

In its weekly newsletter, the American Medical Association told the public how to obtain an "information kit," compiled by the National Agricultural Chemicals Association, to answer questions provoked by *Silent Spring.*

Time magazine called *Silent Spring* "unfair, one-sided, and hysterically over-emphatic." It accused Carson of frightening the public with "emotion-fanning words" and claimed her text was filled with "oversimplifications and downright errors."

Former secretary of agriculture Ezra Taft Benson wrote to Dwight D. Eisenhower regarding Rachel Carson, asking simply "why a spinster with no children was so concerned about genetics." His theory was that she was "probably a Communist."

Spinster. Communist. A member of a nature cult. An amateur naturalist who should stick to poetry and not politics. These were just some of the labels used to discredit her. Rachel Carson had, in fact, lit a fire on America's chemical landscape.

In speeches before the Garden Club of America and the New England Wildflower Preservation Society, Carson fought back against her detractors and addressed her audiences with great passion: "I recommend you to ask yourself — who speaks? And why?" And then again, "Are we being sentimental when we care whether the robin returns to our dooryard and the veery sings in the twilight woods? A world that is no longer fit for wild plants, that is no longer graced by the flight of birds, a world whose streams and forests are empty and lifeless is not likely to be a fit habitat for man himself, for these things are symptoms of an ailing world."

President John F. Kennedy became aware of *Silent Spring* when the book was serialized in the pages of *The New Yorker.* At a press conference on August 29, 1962, a reporter asked Kennedy about the growing concern among scientists about the dangerous long-term side effects of the use of DDT and other pesticides and whether or not the Department of Agriculture or the Public Health Service was planning to launch an investigation into the matter. "Yes," the president replied. "I think particularly, of course, since Miss Carson's book."

The Life Sciences Panel of the President's Science Advisory Committee was charged with reviewing pesticide use. In 1962 the committee issued a call for legislative measures to safeguard the health of the land and its people against pesticides and industrial toxins. The president's report had vindicated Carson. Her poetics were transformed into public policy.

On June 4, 1963, Rachel Carson testified for more than forty minutes during hearings on "Interagency Coordination in Environmental Hazards (Pesticides)" held by a subcommittee of the Senate Committee on Government Operations. According to her biographer Linda Lear, "Those who heard Rachel Carson that morning did not see a reserved or reticent woman in the witness chair but an accomplished scientist, a brilliant writer, and a woman of conscience who made the most of an opportunity few citizens of any rank can have to make their opinions known. Her witness had been equal to her vision." Alaska's Senator Gruening said that *Silent Spring* was equal to *Uncle Tom's Cabin* in its impact and predicted that it would change the course of history.

In 1967, five years after *Silent Spring* was published, the Environmental Defense Fund was born, with a mandate, in the words of one of its founders, "to build a body of case law to establish a citizen's right to a clean environment." Three years after that, in 1970, the Environmental Protection Agency was established. And today we have a new generation of individuals carrying the torch of vigilance forward in the name of ecological integrity, including local heroes like Lois Gibbs, who exposed the Love Canal to the American public as a dark example of industry's arrogance and disregard for the health of communities.

Gibbs's story is just one in an anthology of thousands. How many towns like Times Beach, Missouri, have had to be evacuated because toxicity levels have been so high they have imperiled the people living there? Women such as Monica Moore and Sarojeni Rengah of Pesticide Action Network provide scientific data and policy proposals worldwide to citizens fighting to maintain the biological health of their communities. Women like Mary O'Brien in Eugene, Oregon, remind us that the risk-assessment question "How much of this pesticide is 'safe' or 'acceptable'?" is the wrong question to be asking. The better question is "How much pesticide use is essential?"

These are the green patriots who have taken the banner that Rachel Carson held high and kept it flying in a world that still refuses to believe in the dangers of biocide.

Tyrone Hayes, the lead researcher of a study that concluded that atrazine, the most popular herbicide in the United States, causes a wide range of sexual abnormalities in frogs, was quoted in the *New York Times* on April 17, 2002, as saying, "I'm not saying it's unsafe for humans. All I'm saying is it makes hermaphrodites of frogs."

As Rachel Carson noted, "If . . . we have concluded that we are being asked to take senseless and frightening risks, then we should no longer accept the counsel of those who tell us that we must fill our world with poisonous chemicals; we should look about and see what other course is open to us."

Pam Zahoran of Protect Environment and Children Everywhere is showing us an alternative course. She, along with twenty-two thousand other citizens, signed a petition against a major hazardous waste incinerator to be built by Waste Technologies Industries in East Liverpool, Ohio. Individuals can and do make a difference. We are not powerless. This is the bedrock of democracy — the greatest good for the greatest number for the longest time.

And then there is Robert Boone, president of the Anacostia Watershed Society, who is working with the children of a poverty-stricken community just outside Washington, D.C., to clean up the Anacostia River, one of the most toxic waterways in America, and restore hope to this forgotten landscape. So far they have removed 327 tons of debris, including 7,218 tires, and mobilized 25,666 volunteers to achieve their vision of a clean river. They are holding the Environmental Protection Agency accountable to the provisions of the Clean Water Act.

These are Rachel Carson's sons and daughters, who are taking the facts and fueling them with passionate resistance to preserve the health and integrity of our hometowns and communities.

Rachel Carson reminds us of what it means to be a warrior with heart. In a letter to a friend she wrote, "No, I myself never thought the ugly facts would dominate, and I hope they don't. The beauty of the living world I was trying to save has always been uppermost in my mind — that, and anger at the senseless, brutish things that were being done. I have felt bound by a solemn obligation to do what I could — if I didn't at least try I could never again be happy in nature."

Not long ago I visited the Rachel Carson National Wildlife Refuge, a rich salt marsh that encompasses approximately 4,500 acres along 45 miles of coastline in southern Maine. Carson knew this country well. It was the place she loved most, the place where she spent summers at her cottage near Boothbay Harbor with her nephew, Roger, and her dear soulmate, Dorothy Freeman, who lived nearby.

As I walked through the sanctuary and listened to the water songs of red-winged blackbirds and watched the deliberate flight of blue herons, I wondered: if Carson were alive today, would she find this estuary a bit quieter than it used to be? Would she find the tide pools less vibrant, empty of certain creatures? I wonder what accommodations we have made through time without even noting what we have lost. I would love to ask her what price she paid, personally, for being a warrior over *Silent Spring.*

I can imagine her looking directly into my eyes, a bit stunned, at such a presumptuous question, shaking her head, and then looking out toward her beloved sea. "What choice do we have?"

Rachel Carson died of breast cancer on April 14, 1964,

at the age of fifty-six. The irony is a painful one. Diagnosed in 1960, she wrote *Silent Spring* through her illness and faced powerful opposition with limited physical strength, often having to be hospitalized after meeting strenuous professional obligations. But the public never knew. She proceeded with great presence and resolve, even completing, a few months before her death, a rigorous television interview on CBS, where she was paired with a spokesperson from the chemical industry. Carson's grace under fire with compelling facts to back her sentiments finally won public opinion over to her side. In his column in the *New York Times*, Brooks Atkinson proclaimed her the winner of the debate. He wrote, "Evidence continues to accumulate that she is right and that *Silent Spring* is the 'Rights of Man' of this generation."

Sandra Steingraber, the author of *Living Downstream: An Ecologist Looks at Cancer and the Environment*, writes, "Carson laid out five lines of evidence linking cancer to environmental causes . . . [She] predicted that the full maturation of whatever seeds of malignancy have been sown by the new lethal agents of the chemical age would occur in the years to come."

In spite of her cancer, Rachel Carson never lost the "vision splendid before my eyes." Her love of the natural world, especially all she held dear in the coastal landscape of Maine, sustained her, giving her uncommon strength and peace.

Before her death, she wrote to her friend E. B. White, "It is good to know that I shall live on even in the minds of many who do not know me and largely through association with things that are beautiful and lovely."

And she does.

Consider these references: *Rachel's Daughters*, a film about the environmental causes of breast cancer, and Rachel's Network, a political organization committed to seeing women in positions of power and leadership within the conservation community. There are thousands of other references to Rachel Carson in American culture, including one by a puzzled Richard A. Posner, who wondered in his book *Public Intellectuals* why Rachel Carson had more citations in LexisNexis than the French deconstructionist Jacques Derrida.

What a perfect metaphor for Rachel Carson's impact. After all, didn't she deconstruct the entire chemical industry until we were able to see, collectively, the essence of what it was trying to do — destroy natural systems — and expose the dark toxic roots of pesticides?

And she continues to guide us. Recently, a broad coalition of scientists, environmentalists, feminists, health-care workers, religious leaders, political leaders, philosophers, and writers signed an open letter to the U.S. Senate to ban reproductive cloning and place a moratorium on therapeutic cloning. If Rachel Carson were alive, her name would have appeared on that list.

Similar political actions have been taken over the dangers of genetic engineering, ranging from the possible infection of wild salmon populations to the perils of genetically modified foods. Rachel Carson understood that tampering with nature is tampering with health in the broadest, ecological sense.

In 2002, I want to remember Rachel Carson's spirit. I want it to be both fierce and compassionate at once. I want to carry a sense of indignation inside to shatter the complacency that has seeped into our society. Call it sacred rage, a rage that is grounded in the knowledge that all life is intertwined. I want to know the grace of wild things that sustains hope.

Can we find the moral courage to step forward and openly question every law, person, and practice that denies justice toward nature? Can we continue in this American tradition of bearing witness, which is its own form of advocacy?

Rachel Carson's name is synonymous with courage. She dared to expose the underbelly of the chemical industry and how that industry was disrupting the balance of nature. In *Silent Spring* we see her signature strength as a writer who understands that a confluence of poetry and politics creates an ethics of place. But perhaps Carson's true courage lies in her willingness to align science with the sacred, to admit that her bond toward nature is a spiritual one:

> I am not afraid of being thought a sentimentalist when I say that I believe natural beauty has a necessary place in the spiritual development of any individual or any society. I believe that whenever we destroy beauty, or whenever we substitute something manmade and artificial for a natural feature of the earth, we have retarded some part of man's spiritual growth.

I think of that day with my grandmother, feeding the birds. And I think of that "town in the heart of America where all life seemed to live in harmony with its surroundings." Today the idea of a spring without birdsong is indeed imaginable.

Rachel Carson has called us to action. *Silent Spring* is a social critique of our modern way of life. Consider her closing paragraph:

> The "control of nature" is a phrase conceived in arrogance, born of the Neanderthal age of biology and philosophy, when it was supposed that nature exists for the convenience of man . . . It is our alarming misfortune that so primitive a science has armed itself with the most modern and terrible weapons, and that in turning them against the insects it has also turned them against the earth.

May the new readers of this fortieth edition of *Silent Spring* hear its ongoing prayer to the next generation. We can live differently. We can see the world whole, even holy. The health of the planet is our own. And may the seasoned readers of Rachel Carson return to this book with renewed vows to walk gently on this beloved earth, to remain forever vigilant on behalf of life. Rachel Carson's words remain as sacred text.

FREEMAN HOUSE

Silent Future: Rachel Carson and the Creeping Apocalypse

IT MUST HAVE BEEN in 1970, when I was working with a collective fishing venture in Trinidad, California, that Rachel Carson enrolled me into the school of ecological activism. The affairs of the world seemed so hopelessly screwed up then that I had chosen to divorce myself from mainstream culture and work with others to build a world that fit my fallible sense of the proper way to live. We were in the habit of calling our position "building a new culture within the shell of the old." A less friendly observer of our efforts might describe them as an attempt to ignore the grim imperatives of history, and I would not argue.

I did pick up a copy of the *San Francisco Chronicle* once in a while, and in one of them I read of a scientific report that predicted the imminent extinction of brown pelicans in California due to the thinning effect of the insecticide DDT on the eggs of the birds. The article referred to *Silent Spring* and made me realize how much I loved brown pelicans.

The collective had acquired a double-ended Newfoundland dory, a pretty craft that bobbed in the water like an eggshell, narrow at the beam and twenty feet long. It had two sets of oarlocks and a place to step a mast near its center. The boat replaced our noisy and greasy thirty-foot scow, which was powered by an unreliable diesel engine. With the new boat we could row out in the dawn light to the rockfish holes seaward of the stone monoliths that rose out of the water a half mile or so offshore to get some fishing done before the north winds roiled the water at midday. Then we could set sail as we headed for home, skimming into port and luxuriating like people on a cruise. The quiet on the water was wonderful. Where before we had been isolated from ocean life by a dense aural penumbra of engine-howl, now all the lives of the sea came round to investigate. Seals and sea lions followed us as if we were a carnival show; the gulls circled, shrieking about our heads while common murres sped across our bow like very fast windup toys.

In the middle distance always the pelicans. They look like creatures from another age, their oversized heads stretching forward, heads and beaks that from some angles appear larger than their aerodynamic bodies. There is rarely one alone; more often they fly in groups of six to twenty. The flocks act as if they have a single mind, so precise and graceful are their formations. The pelicans fly most often in a line, one behind the other, the line rising and then plunging thrillingly close to the water's surface in rolling arcs that resemble drawings of a sine wave. But sometimes the birds fly in marvelously sinuous gathered formations, group mind and individual mind working in perfect harmony. The individuals within the group might glide past one another or fall back a bit, but the formation as a whole holds its shape as a mutable polygon, sometimes wheeling in a ninety-degree turn, all white bellies exposed at once, to change direction. It is enough to make you forget the cuts on your hands and live for a moment in the perfect realm of the whole.

It was tempting to think that the birds were tracing arabesques against the looming fog bank merely to pleasure our senses, but the pelicans were fishing, too. Perhaps the varieties of formations represented different strategies for different prey. At the sight of a fish, all semblance of group mind evaporated as one bird after another dropped in twisting free fall, most of them entering the water headfirst with the perfect verticality of a practiced diver. But some birds bellyflop with a huge commotion that can only be described as clumsy. It will take a few moments of shaking the water off their wings and reorienting themselves for the birds to recover their dignity. The sight would make me laugh out loud with empathy, remembering my own equally indecorous moments.

Any bird that can move you to awe and seconds later make you laugh out loud has intrinsic value enough to burn. I was enraged that a bunch of mad utopians out to rid the world of insects that fit into no economic scheme was inflicting the collateral damage of depriving the world of pelicans. And that is how Rachel Carson, several steps removed, influenced a sense of myself as an ecological being, a reciprocal participant in the surrounding world. It was a sense that would inform the rest of my life.

My mother was born within a few years of Rachel Carson, and I was brought up in a time of duck-and-cover drills and visits to check out our neighbors' fallout bunkers. In high school, my anxieties were centered not on girls or grades so much as on the Korean War draft I would face the moment I graduated.

Herman Kahn's *On Thermonuclear War*, a book that calculates human disaster with cold dispassion, had been published in 1960, just two years before Carson's *Silent Spring*. The passion with which Carson applied her dire warnings about the widespread use of pesticides was no doubt fueled in part by a parallel and widely shared dread of nuclear war. Interestingly, both DDT and atomic weaponry were products of World War II. The dangers of DDT first caught Carson's attention in 1945 when, in her capacity as director of publications for the Fish and Wildlife Service, she read classified papers documenting the unanticipated side effects of chemical pesticides on birds and beneficial insects. The "triumph of democracy" had not come without its costs. What Carson couldn't know in 1962 is that the vehicles of destruction were only in second gear.

Shifting to a higher gear, the chemical industry would

continue to develop toxins for the broadcast elimination of insects and go on to develop defoliants to rid the world of plants that didn't pay their way, poisons like dioxin — an ingredient in the infamous Agent Orange, which triggered my brother's Parkinson's disease when he was only thirty-five. The Eisenhower administration's program for an enormous interstate highway system would do its share to accelerate global climate change. Neverending research and development of weapons of war, such as explosives laced with depleted uranium, would make the accelerating practice of war ever more devastating. One fishery after another would disappear due to overfishing; our forests would be fragmented at an alarming pace; and extinctions of whole species would accelerate at an unprecedented rate. Public reaction to the news of the world would sink inexorably from dread into despair.

During the same period, however, another historical engine was beginning to hum. While the concept of ecology goes back to the late nineteenth century, that body of ideas was rarely discussed outside limited scientific circles by the 1950s. It is not too large a stretch to credit Rachel Carson, with the publication of *The Sea Around Us* in 1951, and her contemporary Aldo Leopold with making available to the popular mind for the first time the ideas of the interconnectedness of living processes. Carson's extrapolations burst on the public mind all at once; Leopold's more explicitly moral interpretations would not be "discovered" by the public for some years to come. The degree to which the idea of interconnectedness was new to the lay reader can be demonstrated through my own experience. When I spent a year in the forestry school at Oregon State College in 1955, I don't remember hearing the word *ecology* spoken even once.

Since that time, I haven't been alone in adopting ecology as a lens of perception through which to view the living world. Ecological thinking is now taught in elementary schools. A generation of parents has endured having their food and transportation habits critiqued by their ten-year-olds. Ideas that change the ways that people experience themselves travel along mysterious paths. While writing this essay, I made it a point to quiz people a generation or more younger than I about what they know about Rachel Carson. Most know that the name *should* be familiar to them, but they can't quite place it. When I told one of my brightest and best-educated young friends about my project, she responded, "Oh, yeah, the nuclear disarmament lady." Almost without exception, however, the people I quizzed shuddered at the thought of putting any sort of chemical fertilizer in their kitchen gardens. They buy organic when they can afford it; they are likely to describe themselves as environmentalists and to keep a close watch on the sources and levels of their consumption. Some are building their first homes themselves. They approach the task as students of sustainability, studying the angles of the sun at the worksite, carefully calculating the ways of taking their comforts from what the sun and the earth generously delivers without seriously diminishing it. They look for recycled or local building materials. Among these young people, Rachel Carson's generous and gracefully expressed ideas are becoming anonymously tangible.

As a high-profile social and political movement, the ecological movement since 1970 is easier to track, and numerous scholarly works have been devoted to that subject. There is hardly a nation that doesn't have an environmental agency ostensibly regulating the effects of development. The environmental movement, after a long and successful effort to establish itself as a powerful part of various legal systems, has seen the rise of a second wave: innumerable community organizations devoted to the ecological health and food security of their particular locales. The degree to which such movements have tempered environmental destruction may never be quantifiable, but no one will argue that they have not been significant.

That Rachel Carson knew exactly what she was doing and to whom she was speaking can be demonstrated from this passage in *Silent Spring:*

> For each of us, as for the robin in Michigan or the salmon in the Miramichi, this is a problem of ecology, of interrelationships, of interdependence. We poison the caddis flies in a stream and the salmon runs dwindle and die. We poison the gnats in a lake and the poison travels from link to link of the food chain and soon the birds of the lake margins become victims. We spray our elms and the following springs are silent of robin songs, not because we sprayed the robins directly but because the poison trav-

eled, step by step, through the now familiar elm leaf-earthworm-robin cycle. Theses are matters of record, observable, part of the visible world around us. They reflect the web of life — or death — that scientists know as ecology.

2.

Unlike the little collective described earlier, Rachel Carson faced history boldly. All of her writings share the quality of a brave attempt to *reform* historical drift by guiding her readers toward a love of the natural world, the effect of which she hoped would reduce their rapacity and move them in the direction of once more becoming a respectful part of that world. In each of her books Rachel Carson goes against the grain of the dominant culture, and she does it large. Her first and most lyrical book, *Under the Sea-Wind*, published in 1941, disappeared in America's preoccupation with Pearl Harbor. *The Sea Around Us* (1951) made Carson an instant celebrity, a fact that startled both her publisher and her. And it *was* truly a startling phenomenon. *The Sea Around Us* is not an easy book. Graceful stylistically, it nevertheless requires of the reader an appetite for an avalanche of detail, discussing in some depth cycles and creatures of which most readers had never heard and certainly had almost never related to as important information for the conduct of their daily lives. The excerpts published in *The New Yorker* as a three-part profile certainly contributed to the book's success. But still.

Linda Lear, Carson's devoted biographer, offers a line of speculation to explain the public appetite for such a book. Lear pored over Carson's fan mail received after the publication of *The Sea Around Us*. There she found an audience that, only recently relieved of the anxieties of World War II, found themselves attacked by a new and less clear-cut set of worries: an international nuclear arms race, a witch hunt for domestic Communists, and the prospect of sending their sons to a war in Korea with little understanding of what that war was about. The correspondence often expressed gratitude for giving the reader a broader perspective on the natural world that transcended the ambiguities of the daily news. Lear quotes directly from some of that mail: "We have been troubled about the world, and had almost lost faith in man; it helps to think about the long history of the earth, and of how life came to be. When we think in terms of millions of years, we are not so impatient that our own problems be solved tomorrow." Such sentiments might have been written yesterday.

As eminent an authority as Edward O. Wilson, in his introduction to the 2002 edition of *Silent Spring*, traces a direct line of cause and effect between that book and the U.S ban on DDT in 1972 and the formation of the Environmental Protection Agency in 1970. (In Carson's testimony to Congress in 1963, she had called for just such an agency.)

It's comforting to a writer such as myself to think that a single book can alter the course of the future, and Rachel Carson wrote a couple of them. Back in the 60s and 70s, when things somehow seemed simpler, I sometimes found myself saying, "What we need is a new Karl Marx." What I meant was that someone needed to articulate a paradigm shift that would replace the dialectics of capitalism and communalism, poverty and wealth, war and peace. I was longing for a powerful book that contained a new perception of the real world based on ecology and human identity rather than on global supply and demand. I suppose I still entertained the illusion that a single book — like *Das Kapital* or *Silent Spring* — *could* alter the course of history. A generation later, it is difficult to imagine that any single book could deal with the complexities faced by the planet and its inhabitants.

What if Rachel Carson had lived a longer life? How might she have responded to the creeping apocalypse we call the twenty-first century? Had she somehow been able to maintain the indomitable spirit and energy that allowed her to complete *Silent Spring* while suffering from debilitating health problems, attacks by the chemical industry, and the scorn of all but a few important biologists, it is a good bet that she would have felt driven toward a companion to *The Sea Around Us* with an equally informative book about the earth's atmosphere. Certainly, with her extensive network of contacts within the scientific community, her interest would have been piqued by the data on carbon dioxide levels in the atmosphere that began to emerge from the NASA observatory on Mauna Loa in 1958.

Carson had been half-prescient when she wrote, circa 1950,

> But for the present, the evidence that the top of the world is growing warmer is to be found on every hand. The recession of the northern glaciers is going on at such a rate that many smaller ones have already disappeared. If the present rate of melting continues others will soon follow.

I say half-prescient because she attributed the trend only to cyclical changes documented by the Swedish oceanographer Otto Pettersson in 1912. The chapter in *The Sea Around Us* from which this passage is taken, titled "The Global Thermostat," also gives Carson a claim to being the first popular ecological historian. Had she lived but a few years longer, it is likely that she would have joined, or even led, the shift in the scientific paradigm that began to view the human species since the Industrial Revolution as having had as large an impact on planetary processes as any geological or climatic cycles. Perhaps a book called something like *The Air Around Us* might have come out of that — and perhaps it would have been published in 1980, one of the last years, before the availability of the personal computer, that books would retain their dominance as a source of authoritative information. Would Ronald Reagan have been as receptive a president as Jack Kennedy had been when *Silent Spring* was published? Who knows? Rachel Carson was a very convincing writer.

Donald Worster's magisterial 1977 history of ecological thought, *Nature's Economy*, claims that "the age of ecology" began in 1945 with the realization that technology had reached the point of having the capacity to destroy all life. He recognizes Rachel Carson's role as the midwife of concepts of ecology in the popular mind. "The truly unique feature of the Age of Ecology," he goes on to claim, "was its sense of nature as a defenseless victim."

From the perspective of late 2006, I would make the claim that the "Age of Ecology" is actually beginning just about now. For more than twenty years, a manufactured debate about the effect of human technologies on carbon dioxide levels in the atmosphere has diverted us from the direct observations of climate change available during the same time. So successfully has a handful of hired scientists propped up one side of the argument with claims of inadequate evidence that the small part of the human population that controls the larger part of the earth's resources has been able to remain comfortable in its course of ever-increasing consumption and personal entitlement. Worster describes what he calls "the long rise of bourgeois civilization" leading up to his post–1945 Age of Ecology: "the worldview of the aspiring middle class, with its dedication to technology, unlimited production and consumption, self-advancement, individualism, and the domination of nature." He writes that "time had run out on these modern-age values: nature's economy had been pushed to the breaking point, and 'ecology' was to be the rallying cry of the revolution." Worster's analysis strikes me as entirely accurate, but his message was heard by too small a segment of the late-twentieth-century postindustrial society. (The fact that 1980, three years after the publication of *Nature's Economy*, was when regional planner Mathis Wackernagel, now head of the Global Footprint Network, published his calculations that the rate of increase of human consumption of natural resources had outstripped the ability of the earth to maintain it is either an interesting coincidence or a validation of Worster's insight.)

As I write, the dam of denial regarding humanly influenced climate change seems to be breaching. Nature can no longer be viewed as "a defenseless victim" but must be dealt with on its own terms. Humans no longer have the luxury of *thinking* about ecology in the abstract; we are living it. Climate prediction models must be updated nearly weekly to keep pace with newly observed positive feedback loops, such as the realization that the melting tundra of the Northern Hemisphere is perhaps the second-largest carbon sink on the planet (second to the world ocean) and that global thaw will release carbon into the atmosphere at a rate comparable to that released by fossil fuel emissions. Entire villages in the Polynesian and Aleutian islands are being considered for relocation, canaries in the atmospheric coal mine.

As a person who has spent the majority of his adult life working toward salmon and watershed recovery in a single small river basin, I have had to face the fact that during the whole of that time my coworkers and I have never allowed the prospect of climate change into our ever-evolving strategies. I had been a stone in that dam of denial even as I had so freely denounced others for their insouciance. In the July 13, 2006, issue of the *New York Review of Books*, Jim

Hansen, the director of the Goddard Institute for Space Studies, lined out a best- and a worst-case scenario for the inevitabilities of climate change as ranging between a two- to five-degree Fahrenheit increase in average global temperatures. When I recently researched my region's climatological history for a book I was working on, I learned that the last time the local air temperature was two degrees warmer, a mere five to six thousand years ago, there were few if any salmon using northwestern California's rivers. If Hansen's projections are accurate, then what can we mean by ecological restoration? What might we be restoring but the human capacity to live within nature? My neighbors and I had been working for twenty-five years as if the ecological systems in which we were immersed were the once and always landscape, rather than a fluid system of systems that respond harmonically to global conditions over time beyond the capacity of human memory to grasp.

The biosphere arranges itself into a marvelous array of bioregions, each of which will react differently to climate change based on its location. Proximity to the world's oceans, location in reference to the poles, forest cover, biological diversity, and human impact will each determine the way that climate change will affect various bioregions. Such diversity alone would eliminate the likelihood of a single book, even under the graceful hand of a Rachel Carson, spelling out strategies for an adaptive future. For adaptation is the name of the game. As in prehistoric times, other creatures are once more leading the way, giving us signals of what lies ahead. Jim Hansen reports that

> [d]uring the last thirty years the lines marking the regions in which a given average temperature prevails ("isotherms") have been moving poleward at a rate of about thirty-five miles per decade. That is the size of a county in Iowa. Each decade the range of a given species is moving one row of counties northward.

Human communities face even larger challenges than those of other species as their habitats change.

Once DDT was banned, brown pelican populations rebounded. In my own river system, salmon seem to have responded to our ministrations. We have played a part in the survival of one of the last half-dozen strains of totally native Chinook in California for at least a while longer, perhaps to recolonize nearby rivers where those fish have been lost. But for the past two years, the seasonal upwelling of cold water from the deep that provides essential nutrients to sea-dependent creatures has failed, and there are reports of pelican starvation farther south along our California coast. The populations of rockfish that I had once heedlessly thought would feed me forever have crashed and are sinking even lower as a result of the failed upwelling. Differentials in ocean and air temperatures are known to drive the great ocean currents, and speculation abounds as to whether or not we are seeing yet another symptom of climate change. It is too soon to tell.

Regional responses to climate change continue to represent the most positive current strategies in response to the inevitability of the changes to come. Municipal, regional, and state governments, often driven by grass-roots organizations, abound with adaptive and innovative changes to their infrastructures. There is a desperation in these activities, a sure knowledge that they will not be enough in the absence of national and international leadership and cooperation. Rarely do local coalitions include the practitioners of agribusiness and industry who have so much to do with the ways we live. There is no local constituency for the world ocean or the atmosphere.

If global capitalism has denatured nationalism and ethnic identity, climate change is likely to trump globalism, replacing it as the context in which socioeconomic phenomena is perceived. Jared Diamond writes in *Collapse* of the elements that have undermined past societies: deforestation and habitat destruction, soil problems, water management problems, overhunting, overfishing, effects of introduced species on native species, human population growth, and increased per capita impact of humans. If any of these items haven't been mentioned in this essay, you can read about them in almost any daily newspaper. The world has changed since Rachel Carson's time. The human population has doubled, and information and complexity have grown at exponential rates. Faith-driven stateless terrorists have successfully raised the stakes on state terrorism by adding a new dimension of uncertainty and universal fear. New plagues have appeared and we can expect more: AIDS, avian flu, the West Nile virus. Life on earth will change and nowhere is there a mind or a bank of computers that can predict just how it will change, and where.

I find myself thinking a lot about chaos theory, another lens through which to view the phenomenal world, also developed since 1963. In chaos theory, the natural order of living systems is to increase in complexity to the point that the infrastructure that has constituted reality undergoes a sudden shift into "emergent properties," forms that don't necessarily resemble the forms we have known before. The theory can be demonstrated on blue screens using computer models. Emergent properties are unpredictable but they seem to be a function of ongoing Creation. Sometimes I'm able to sustain some serenity by using this lens, because ongoing Creation is the lodestone of my faith. It is not the proofs on a computer screen that sustain me, though, but the ideas that Carson did so much to make available to us: that each one of us is connected to the whole and that our actions — especially those actions magnified by their practice in community and society — matter.

To keep my spirits up, I keep a recent clipping from the *San Francisco Chronicle* pinned on my wall that reminds me that there is still so much that we do not know, and over which we have no control: "Huge solar storms could zap Earth, scientists say." There is nothing in chaos theory that postulates that emergent properties will include the survival of human life. There is also nothing in the concept that precludes a critical mass of humanity coming awake one morning to experience themselves as fleshy embodiments of the biosphere with standards of ethics pulsing between the twin ideals of social justice and ecological health. It is an axiom that we cannot predict with any accuracy the effect of our actions. The information with which we are flooded becomes white (or black) noise, and the future is silent.

ROBERT MICHAEL PYLE

Always a Naturalist

DURING MY FIRST YEARS of college, attempting to major in natural history in a hard-biology department, I trolled the secondhand bookshops up and down University Avenue in Seattle for any nature books I could afford. These were usually thumbed-through paperbacks with turned-down pages and broken spines, but they still worked: they could still be read. I picked up everything from Sterling North's *Rascal* to Marston Bates's *The Forest and the Sea; King Solomon's Ring* by Konrad Lorenz; and *Curious Naturalists* by his mentor, Niko Tinbergen. After a quick read I boxed up many of these books and sent them to my mother, who shared my interests, in Denver. When I visited her the following summer, I would bring them back to Seattle, along with other titles she'd gathered from used bookstores on Colfax Avenue, to bolster my growing horde of natural history books: antidote to mathematical biology, counterbalance to my chemistry textbooks.

The last time I visited Mom, in the summer of 1967, she was reluctant to let go of all the books I intended to take back. "Won't you leave me any?" she pled, and I realized that my greed was overwhelming my sensitivity for her own needs. Besides my shame at that moment, what I remember most clearly are the books that caused my mother to let me know how she really felt: her Rachel Carsons. She so loved *The Edge of the Sea*, *The Sea Around Us*, and *Under the Sea-Wind* that my presumption in removing them triggered her tearful outburst. On reflection, I am not surprised that these were the books that mattered most. Rachel Carson once wrote that "it isn't at all surprising that I should have written a book about the sea, because as long as I can remember it has fascinated me. Even as a child — long before I had ever seen it — I used to imagine what it would look like, and what the surf sounded like." So it was for my mother. She grew up in Seattle, came to love the seaside best, but moved to Colorado young and always felt marooned there. I caught this condition from her and fled to the coast for college. We schemed that I would eventually help her return to Washington. Meanwhile, along with Anne Morrow Lindbergh's *Gift from the Sea* and Hazel Heckman's *Island in the Sound*, Carson's oceanic trilogy kept her alive. That moment — when she wouldn't let those paperbacks go — may have been the first time I witnessed how much a book, or an author, could really mean to a reader. I left those books with her, of course. But Mom did send me home with another book of Carson's, her final, posthumous title, which had recently been published. *A Sense of Wonder* seemed to speak to everything I was trying to do, and to all my callow but earnest hopes as a young conservationist.

That autumn, in a botany class, I met Thea Peterson, who would become my wife many years later. In our first conversation we discovered that we shared a strong interest in conservation. Thea told me, and still maintains, that *Silent Spring* was the most important book she ever read. "She showed me how I wanted to live my life," Thea said. I ran out and found a copy of *Silent Spring* on the Ave, and quickly saw what she meant. As we and our peers worked on conservation issues as student activists, watched the banning of DDT and other pesticide reforms take place before our eyes, and eventually witnessed the comeback of bald eagles, ospreys, peregrine falcons, and brown pelicans, we thought of Carson. She was an absent patron saint, like Muir, Leopold, and Krutch, and a very present inspiration along with giants still living at the time such as Brower, Abbey, Udall, Douglas, Peterson, Teale, and Mardy Murie.

Much later I learned how Rachel Carson had accidentally become the great public interpreter of the seas. I had the pleasure of hearing the story directly from Paul Brooks, the longtime Houghton Mifflin editor, when my own editor at that house, Harry Foster, took me to meet Brooks not long before he died. Parts of the tale are also recounted in Brooks's intimate portrait of Carson, *This*

House of Life; his literary memoir, *Two Park Street;* and Linda Lear's biography *Rachel Carson: Witness for Nature.* During a weekend house party at Edmond Wilson's Provincetown, Cape Cod, summer home, the great critic, his daughter, Rosalind, and various others were strolling an outer beach. Horseshoe crabs were in, tumbled about in great numbers and crawling over one another. Some of the guests, concerned and thinking them stranded, began tossing the animals back into the water, until one companion explained that they were trying to spawn on shore and the well-meaning guests were interfering with their progress. Someone present lamented the lack of a good book to educate caring but uninformed people about such common life at the seashore. Rosalind Wilson, then an editor at Houghton Mifflin, reported this episode to Paul Brooks the following Monday morning. At that time, Brooks was in discussion with Rachel Carson about a book of historic bird illustrations by Louis Agassiz Fuertes, for which she hoped to write the text, if Houghton would publish it. An admirer of Carson's first, little-known book, *Under the Sea-Wind*, Brooks asked Carson if she might be interested in writing instead such a book about oceanside life. Thus was born *The Edge of the Sea* and, eventually, *Silent Spring.* I love this story, especially the way it illustrates the power and primacy of natural history through Carson's life: how an intimate acquaintance with the natural world is vital not only to living with it, but for informing and motivating environmental conservation. We take this connection for granted now, and it should seem self-evident to any biologist. But prior to Carson, *The Edge of the Sea*, and *Silent Spring*, few really acted on this fact.

I have imagined that the naturalist who knew what the horseshoe crabs were about might have been Vladimir Nabokov, then still a close friend and frequent guest of Wilson's. Though Nabokov did occasionally visit the Wilsons in Provincetown, there is no evidence that Carson and Nabokov had any such oblique connection. Yet in a certain way, I believe Rachel Carson embodied a particularly Nabokovian view of the world. In a *New York Times Book Review* appraisal of a volume on Audubon's paintings of butterflies and moths, Nabokov asked a rhetorical question: "Does there not exist a high ridge, where the mountainside of 'scientific' knowledge meets the opposite slope of 'artistic' imagination?" I say rhetorical, because such an ambidextrous habitat is exactly the territory Nabokov occupied. As both an accomplished (and still admired) lepidopterist and one of the greatest fiction writers ever in two languages, Nabokov knew full well that an individual could thrive in both atmospheres. He professed to be less concerned about giving his readers too much science than with failing to fully inform his science with his art. He spoke happily of "the precision of poetry and the art of science." Nabokov was not the only scientist of substance who also visited his full intelligence and subtlety upon his literary output — we think of Goethe, Loren Eiseley, and Lewis Thomas — but I know of no one who strode that rarefied ridge as sure-footedly as Rachel Carson. This was no accident; in fact, it was part of her own credo. In her acceptance speech at the National Book Awards ceremony in 1952, she challenged "the notion that 'science' is something that belongs in a separate compartment of its own, apart from everyday life." She said that "the aim of science is to discover and illuminate truth. And that, I take it, is the aim of literature, whether biography or history or fiction. It seems to me, then, that there can be no separate literature of science." This accords with my own view that the term *nature writing* is a redundancy.

Unlike Nabokov, Carson walked the ridge between art and science as a writer of essay, where the distinction between reflection and refraction is even muddier than in fiction and requires even greater rigor to maintain. Yet her values, lyricism, metaphor, and poetry never degrade or detract from her wealth of deeply informed fact. "My own guiding principle," she said in that 1952 address, "was to portray the subject of my sea profile with fidelity and understanding. All else was secondary. I did not stop to consider whether I was doing it scientifically or poetically; I was writing as the subject demanded.

The winds, the sea, and the moving tides are what they are. If there is wonder and beauty and majesty in them, science will discover these qualities. If they are not there, science cannot create them. If there is poetry in my book about the sea, it is not because I deliberately put it there, but because no one could write truthfully about the sea and leave out the poetry."

Reviewers agreed. The *New York Herald Tribune* said of *The Sea Around Us* that "it is a work of science; it is stamped with authority. It is a work of art: it is saturated with the excitement of mystery. It is literature." And as *Time* described *The Edge of the Sea*, "again author Carson has shown her remarkable talent for catching the life breath of science on the still glass of poetry." Yet quite apart from the lyrical peace she found in her beloved Maine tide pools, and in writing about them, Rachel Carson also carried her art and her science into a bitterly hostile political arena — something Nabokov assiduously avoided, and for which she was both vilified and lionized, and even called a follower of some "cult of the balance of nature." As Paul Brooks put it, "she was not at heart a crusader. But at last she decided that if it were to be done, she would have to do it herself." So she did, and in consequence, the very health of the earth was changed.

When my college friends and I threw our enthusiasm toward conservation as well as against the Vietnam War, we had every expectation that our efforts and optimism would be rewarded. If not so naïve as to expect ecotopia, we really did believe that the kindly earth could be saved through activism and education. And we had reinforcement in that direction. The North Cascades National Park for which we battled really was created and its high valleys and peaks protected. We kept dams out of the Grand Canyon. While others were marching to take over the president's office and demanding peace and justice, we marched to the former marshland that the university had leased to the city as the Montlake Dump, occupied it, and demanded topsoil and trees; as a result, it has become one of the great urban wildlife habitats. The Wilderness Act, the Clean Air and Clean Water acts, and many other glorious victories ensued. Jimmy Carter doubled the size of the national park system through the Alaska Lands Act, and of course, thanks to Carson, DDT was banned. We had no reason to believe that conservation would not ultimately win the day.

But perhaps we should have read our Paul Ehrlich and Rachel Carson more closely. She suffered from no false hopes. In a 1953 letter to the *Washington Post*, reprinted in *Reader's Digest*, she criticized the Eisenhower administration's sacking of Albert M. Day, a dedicated director of the U.S. Fish and Wildlife Service, and other conservation professionals in favor of patronage hacks. "These actions within the Interior Department fall into place beside the proposed giveaway of our offshore oil reserves and the threatened invasion of national parks, forests, and other public lands," she wrote. Had she lived to see it, she would have been dismayed but not surprised when along came Reagan, Watt, Hodel, and the Sagebrush Rebellion; the *Exxon Valdez*, Bhopal, Love Canal, and Three Mile Island; Bush I, Iraq I, and the Timber Salvage Act; Monsanto (one of Carson's fiercest attackers), ADM, and GM crops like BT corn and Roundup-Ready soybeans; Bush II, Iraq II, and the general attack on the EPA and all other environmental fronts. In light of our current environmental dark age, where the "war on the land" masquerades as the "war on terror," the way Carson ended that letter could not be more eerily prescient: "It is one of the ironies of our time that, while concentrating on the defense of our country against enemies from without, we should be so heedless of those who would destroy it from within."

Another tragic irony of environmental history was that Rachel Carson herself perished young from a kind of cancer that has proliferated to plague proportions in the organophosphate era that she helped hold back. Along with Peak Oil, global climate change, and a population of 300 million Americans have come thousands of new chemicals on the market, and cancer swarms in numbers undreamed of in Carson's day. Maybe the indicators — robins dead on the lawn, ospreys cracking their own eggshells — aren't as obvious this time around. But the number of toxins released into our air, soil, and waters is greater than ever, and the amoral chemical combines show no compunction over this condition. We can't be sure that any given cancer belongs to the legacy of our toxic load, but it is beyond reason to imagine that many do not. When my wife, Thea, confronted ovarian cancer several years ago, she might have owed it to any number of factors. And beyond question, her recovery stands in debt to intensive modern chemistry involving derivatives of natural substances such as taxol and platinum. For this I am intensely grateful. But that we are forced into a Faustian contract involving sophisticated chemical fixes for the sour fruits of an ever-more chemicalized world strikes me as an unacceptable tradeoff. The hopes of current and future sufferers of a polluted planet owe largely to this one woman who affected great change.

But the sad fact is that forty-five years after the publication of *Silent Spring*, we need Rachel Carson more than ever.

In Shepherdstown, West Virginia, stands the National Conservation Training Center of the U.S. Fish and Wildlife Service, Rachel Carson's one-time employer. This magnificent facility, all stone and wood and set in a campus of woods and meadows, has three dormitories. These are named for great figures in wildlife conservation: Ding Darling, Aldo Leopold, and Rachel Carson. Hers is a name that will never be forgotten, wherever anyone so much as thinks of conservation. And her gentle, percipient presence is a judgment upon all who would wreak enormities upon the land, air, soil, water, and sea. Especially the sea. How her own views evolved on the ocean's future should instruct us all. In a 1942 letter to her publicist describing the general plan of her first sea book, *Under the Sea-Wind*, Carson wrote, "The ocean is too big and vast and its forces are too mighty to be much affected by human activity." But by 1960, in view of the dumping of nuclear wastes at sea, she had changed her mind. In her preface that year for the revised edition of *The Sea Around Us*, she said that "although man's record as a steward of natural resources of the earth has been a discouraging one, there has long been a certain comfort in the belief that the sea, at least, was inviolate, beyond man's ability to change and to despoil. But this belief, unfortunately, has proved to be naïve." And she concluded: "It is a curious situation that the sea, from which life first arose, should now be threatened by the activities of one form of that life." In this she was sadly right. Absent speedy and radical change, the oceanographer Jeremy Jackson expects an impoverished, slimy soup, inhabited chiefly by a monoculture of adaptive jellies called salps, to replace the hugely diverse wonderlands described in Carson's books.

Just as she arrived at an understanding of how we are harming the high seas themselves, Rachel Carson intuited the reality of global climate change. As she wrote to Dorothy Freeman,

> It was pleasant to believe, for example, that much of Nature was forever beyond the tampering reach of man — he might level the forests and dam the streams, but the clouds and the rain and the wind were God's — the God of your ice-crystal cathedral in that beautiful passage of a recent letter of yours.
>
> It was comforting to suppose that the stream of life would flow on through time in whatever course that God had appointed for it — without interference by one of the drops of the stream — man. And to suppose that, however the physical environment might mold Life, that Life could never assume the power to change things drastically — or even destroy — the physical world.

But she was coming to know better. Climate change was one of several subjects she might have pursued in depth, had her time not run out. She even anticipated, slightly slant, the title of Al Gore's film on the subject, *An Inconvenient Truth.* In a speech to the National Women's Press Club in 1962, having cited the monetary control that chemical companies exercise over pesticide research results, she asked this: "Is industry becoming a screen through which facts must be filtered, so that the hard, uncomfortable truths are kept back and only the harmless morsels allowed to filter through?" And Carson's shift in understanding went well beyond anticipating the critically injured seas and skies of today. She began to see the capacity of her species to actually endanger itself. "But the sea," she wrote, "though changed in a sinister way, will continue to exist; the threat is rather to life itself."

It was life, after all, that ultimately enthralled Rachel Carson, in all its ways of being. Brooks's biography, *The House of Life*, is well named. Above all, Carson was always a naturalist. This shows in her long, warm friendships with Edwin and Nellie Teale, Roger Tory Peterson, and others who built their lives largely around a passion for animals, plants, and habitats beyond the strictly human realm. Both Carson and her mother, Marion, benefited from the peak of the American nature-study movement, and it shows throughout her life and work. The maritime books speak for themselves in this regard on every page. But so does almost everything else she wrote. Even the personal letters Carson addressed to her dear friend Dorothy Freeman and other correspondents contain frequent passages describing the texture, color, smell, and inhabitants of her best-beloved places, such as the shore forest in Maine she called the "Lost Woods." From bird walks and tide pool crawls wrested from a busy schedule to the topics of her occasional articles and lectures, close attention to the living world informed Carson's whole being.

Those who identify the writer chiefly with intertidal creatures and DDT are often surprised to discover the breadth of her interests in natural history. I hope I've never defined her in such a narrow way; yet I was recently caught up short by a surprising example of her amplitude as a naturalist. Thea and I had spent an early evening in Portland, Oregon, watching the swirling descent of Vaux's swifts into a tall school chimney where they roost for a fortnight or so during their migration. Like the residents of Austin, Texas, who assemble at dusk to watch the Mexican free-tailed bats fly out from their roost beneath the Congress Street Bridge, locals had gathered with picnic baskets and telescopes, and a festival atmosphere overruled the rain. A Cooper's hawk alighted on the rim of the chimney, scaring off the swirl, and now and then it hopped in and grabbed one of the already alighted swifts. Then it flew off with the sacrifice, while the others resumed their impression of smoke curling into the smokestack backwards. Flying out myself the next morning, I spent the next couple of evenings bewitched by the related chimney swifts screaming through twilight towns in Kansas and Oklahoma, and dropping at last into their night-roost stacks.

Chimney swifts, like the European bird known in England as *the* swift, once must have roosted and nested in hollow trees, prior to the loss of such features from the countryside and the fortunate adaptation of the birds to their anthropogenic alternatives. Vaux's swifts, which still nest largely in hollow trees but often roost in big smokestacks during migration, are beginning to nest in chimneys as well — the first example I heard of took place in my own valley. It occurred to me that we are witnessing the evolution of a western chimney swift in our own time. Coming home, intending to write an essay on these marvelous birds and pretty sure my insight was not wholly original, I searched for any prior observations along these lines. And where did I find the most compelling one? By accident — while working on this piece. Right there in Linda Lear's compilation *Lost Woods: The Discovered Writing of Rachel Carson*, I found Carson's 1944 essay "Aces of Nature's Aviators," on the adaptations and migration of chimney swifts. "Ancestors of the modern chimney swift lived in great hollow trees," she wrote. And "the western cousin of the chimney swift — Vaux's swift — only of recent years has begun to make the transition from trees to chimneys." And "an occasional swift may be snatched by a hawk as the birds are circling above a chimney, preparatory to entering for the night." So there it was — aced by Rachel Carson!

Except one can never be scooped as a naturalist, only anticipated and given shoulders to stand on for the next, farther vantage. Demure as she was, Rachel Carson's shoulders have proved as broad and sturdy as any in all of American natural history. One striking example has arisen recently, with the publication of a book I consider as important as any since *Silent Spring*. I am speaking of Richard Louv's *Last Child in the Woods: Saving Our Children from Nature-Deficit Disorder*. Like Paul Brooks and Rachel Carson with *Silent Spring*, Louv's editor suggested his author's book title — or in this case, the subtitle, which is catching on in a similarly incendiary style. Louv's vital premise is that our culture, and the future of conservation, are being profoundly compromised by the radical loss of everyday contact between children and the outdoors.

Though this baleful condition has never been put so well or so forcefully, Louv's ideas have their antecedents, which he graciously acknowledges. One of the earliest and most resonant of these was Rachel Carson. She first iterated her ideas along these lines in an essay for *Woman's Home Companion* titled "Help Your Child to Wonder." The piece was later expanded and published as a book, with photographs, under the title *A Sense of Wonder*, the book my mother had given me. The phrase "sense of wonder" may be as famous as the term *silent spring*, but relatively few know that they came from the same source. At its heart is Carson's wish that every child in the world have "a sense of wonder so indestructible that it would last throughout life, as an unfailing antidote against the boredom and disenchantments of later years, the sterile preoccupation with things that are artificial, the alienation from the sources of our strength." Richard Louv's book shows chillingly how those very states of preoccupation and alienation have nearly come to pass and suggests ways in which we might get back toward Carson's dream.

I have felt close to this woman for much of my life, and looking over our lives, it's not hard to see why. Like her, I was born far from the sea, yet felt captivated by it. Even the jacket illustration of my 1959 paperback copy of *The Edge of the Sea*, adorned with the bright pink mouth of a king conch, a green crab, a sea star, and a scattering of shells on a golden beach, filled me with longing. When I actually got to the coast of Maine for the summer of 1963, not far from the very shores that she and Dorothy most loved, and three years later to the wilderness beaches of the Olympic Peninsula, Carson's tide pool tales told me who I was seeing, what they were doing, and how to look more deeply beneath the surface of the water, beneath the surface of things as they seemed. Though our experiences were offset by years, I eventually learned that we had shared certain friends, mentors and inspirations, critical boosts, publishers, and convictions. I'd love to have known her. I'd love to have walked a tidal reach with her. Though, like my mother and many others, I almost feel I have.

Maybe I never felt this propinquity more keenly than when I was working on *Chasing Monarchs*, a narrative of following the migration of monarch butterflies. I was reading *Always, Rachel* at the time and came across one of her last letters to Dorothy Freeman, when Carson knew she probably hadn't long to live. Carson had just lost a dear cat and was about to leave her beloved Southport, Maine, likely for the final time. Freeman took her to a favorite place at the end of the island, where they encountered masses of monarchs nectaring on goldenrod. Afterward, Carson wrote to Freeman, "most of all, I shall remember the Monarchs, their unhurried westward drift of one small winged form after another, each drawn by some invisible force." I thought this one of the loveliest descriptions of monarchs I'd ever read, right up there with her contemporary Jo Brewer's wonderful phrase in *Wings on the Meadow:* "these wings of flame, rising to the sun." Carson continued, "We talked a little about their migration, their life history. Did they return? We thought not; for most, at least, this was the closing journey of their lives." Yet this had been "a happy spectacle," she wrote. "And rightly — for when any living thing has come to the end of its life cycle we accept that end as natural. For the Monarch, that cycle is measured in a known span of months. For ourselves, the measure is something else, the span of which we cannot know. But the thought is the same: when the intangible cycle has run its course it is a natural and not unhappy thing that a life comes to its end." She concluded, "That is what these brightly fluttering bits of life taught me this morning. I found a deep happiness in it — so, I hope, may you."

The rest of my mother's books came to me all too soon. Natural cycles or no, her life, like Carson's, ended way too early. Rachel Carson lived from 1907 to 1964; Helen Lee Miller from 1916 to 1967. They were both gifted naturalists and writers. Though their lives largely overlapped, their experiences could hardly have been more different — except for their suffering before they died and their joy when they came under the spell of a shoreline and the central place of natural history in their lives. They never met, yet Rachel Carson kept my mother good company in the last years of her life. An intensely private person always denied much privacy, Rachel Carson was vitally important in millions of lives. She remains so in mine.

LINDA LEAR

Remembrance of Life

"I MAY NOT LIKE what I see," Rachel Carson wrote a friend in December 1958, "but it does no good to ignore it, and it's worse than useless to go on repeating the old 'eternal verities' that are no more eternal than the hills of the poets." And with that no-nonsense appraisal, this brave and gentle writer whose pen provoked a revolution in environmental consciousness made a personal decision to get on with writing about "life in the light of the truth as it now appears to us." That truth she made public in *Silent Spring* — a book of apocalyptic foreboding. It warned us that all might not be well with our world and our love affair with science and technology. It was an angry, damning, often biting description of the consequences of human hubris. But readers who remember Rachel Carson as just another contemporary prophet of doom not only miss the triumphal arc of her journey, but the seamlessness of her vision. In her brief life, Carson moved from unbounded wonder to deep despair at the potential outcome of human domination of the natural world. Rachel Carson, one of the finest writers of English in the twentieth century, was first of all a scientist and a writer who pondered the relationship of life to life. As such, she was forever rooted in possibility, and it is that quality to which she courageously returned at the end of her life, and which gives her work unity and transformative power.

Ironically, all of Carson's literary oeuvre was closely associated with war, human conflict, and the destruction of life. She began her public writing life first as a nature columnist for the *Baltimore Sun*, where she passed herself off as a man to enhance her scientific credibility. Employed as a part-time government biologist and science writer, she had been given the assignment of making fish and their diverse aquatic habitats interesting to the American public. Her research included time onboard a dredging boat that steamed up and down Vineyard Sound from the Woods Hole biological research station. Once a day the dredge would spill its load of sea animals, rocks, shells, and seaweed out on the ship's deck. Carson had never seen, read about, or even imagined some of the creatures strewn at her feet. "They were," she recalled, "dripping with seawater and clinging to a piece of rock or shell or weed that they had brought up from their home down there on the bottom of the sound." And so she let her imagination go down through the water in order to piece together an understanding of "the world as it is known by shore birds and fishes and beach crabs." Over the course of several years in the late 1930s, Carson transformed an eleven-page introduction to a government fisheries brochure into an essay published in the *Atlantic Monthly*, and finally into a book extolling the mysterious and wonderful world that is lived by nonhuman creatures under the sea.

Under the Sea-Wind: A Naturalist's Picture of Ocean Life, published in 1941, considered the shore world of a sanderling, the open-sea life of a mackerel, and finally the varied migrations of an eel from the deep Atlantic abyss to the estuaries of the mid-Atlantic sea coast. Carson assiduously avoided "the viewpoint of the human observer" in her account. "The ocean is too big and vast and its forces are too mighty to be much affected by human activity," she explained. She decided that her story should be told as a simple narrative of the lives of certain animals of the sea. She hoped that her readers would feel as if they were actually living the lives of sea creatures, without human conceptions of time, sound, light, or shelter. Later, she realized that, important as her sea creatures were to the story of life underwater, the ocean itself was her central character. "The smell of the sea's edge, the feeling of vast movements of water, the sound of waves, crept into every page, and over all was the ocean as the force dominating all its creatures."

The publication of *Under the Sea-Wind* went largely unnoticed. The rave reviews Carson had every right to anticipate were muted by the attack on the U.S. Naval base at Pearl Harbor; her lyrical descriptions were obliterated by the sinking of ships and the drowning of men, and the subsequent call to Armageddon. But a few critics noted the arrival of a physical scientist with literary genius. Hers was a new voice in the canon of nature writing, one inspired by delight in the mysterious and the wonderful, and she had the literary skills to dramatize it. *Under the Sea-Wind*, in many ways Carson's most successful book, is a powerful affirmation of life, its continuity, and its immutability. Importantly, it is a book entirely devoid of human activity. "To stand at the edge of the sea," she wrote, "to feel the breath of a mist moving over a great salt marsh, to watch the flight of shore birds that have swept up and down the surf lines for untold millions of years, is to have knowledge of things that are as nearly eternal as any earthly life can be. These things were before ever man stood on the shore of the ocean and looked out upon it with wonder; they continue year in, year out, through the centuries and the ages, while kingdoms rise and fall."

Carson's passion to experience the ocean's secrets herself was difficult to manage, since she was a government bureaucrat tied to a Washington desk. But she took advantage of every opportunity for firsthand observation of tides, waves, and currents. She cleverly maneuvered passage on a government research ship that sailed off the Georges Bank making soundings and exploring the deepest ocean floor. This experience not only brought Carson new treasures from the deep, but it also revealed the unmistakable evidence of overfishing and species extinction. Carson managed as well to get undersea herself, in a brief but memorable dive enclosed in a heavy iron helmet among the kelp beds off the Florida coast. She could not see much, but she experienced what it was like to view the sea's surface above her head. It was enough.

Lacking time and money to finance her own research, the government science writer was compensated by being in an ideal position to study the latest oceanographic reports that flooded across her desk at the U.S. Fish and Wildlife Service. The American public needed no reminders in the postwar years that its physical security and economic future were dependent upon a greater understanding of the surrounding seas that, until 1941, had kept it safe. War had reinforced human dependence not only on oceanographic science and exploration but on the resources of the ocean — "the wealth of the salt seas," as Carson called them.

The publication of *The Sea Around Us*, a decade after her first book, coincided with the onset of another war, this time in far-off Korea. These were uncertain and anxious years. Carson's magisterial synopsis of the creation and life of the ocean exactly captured the public's need for accurate scientific information. She provided the truth about an unknown physical reality: its physics, geology, biology, and ecology, complex science once again made palatable by the poetry of her prose. *The Sea Around Us* was one of the biggest literary successes in publishing history. It was serialized in *The New Yorker*, the first nonfiction piece serialized in that prestigious magazine, and appeared in book form in July 1951. Overnight, Rachel Carson became not just a literary sensation but also a voice of clarity and calm in a world gone mad with new and sometimes sinister technology with the potential for global annihilation.

The leitmotif of all of Carson's work, the long, immutable stream of time, is beautifully set forth in this magisterial account of Oceanus. She did not intend *The Sea Around Us* to be an escape from the immediate perils of contemporary living. She meant instead to call attention to the great realities of life — realities that she still believed were unchangeable: "the mysteries of living things, and the birth and death of continents and seas." Once again humankind has no place in her story, but human activity left an imprint: she observes loss of species, loss of islands, loss of coastline.

The Sea Around Us also contains Carson's first published warning of pollution and evidence of destructive interference in the vast cycles of the ocean. In one chapter, "The Birth of an Island," Carson explains the slow emergence of an island with its unique collection of flora and fauna, describing how it had been transformed by humankind's thoughtless destruction of such fragile habitats. "In a reasonable world," she wrote, "men would have treated these islands as precious possessions, as natural museums filled with beautiful and curious works of creation, valuable beyond price because nowhere in the world are they duplicated." Unhappy at what she had observed, Carson admitted to a friend, "What has taken centuries to develop is being destroyed in a few years."

After 1951, the specter of atomic pollution, not just the

horror of atomic war, laid a shadow across Carson's joyful celebration of life. Pollution caused by human decisions and driven by technology increasingly shaped her vision of the future and reluctantly, but inevitably, moved her to action. By focusing on the immutable forces of nature, *The Sea Around Us* had calmed atomic fears in her readers, but while writing the book, Carson's worldview had been profoundly altered. The Bikini Islands tests in the Pacific, the spread of nuclear arms among the nations, and the stalemate of Korea soon rendered her incapable of claiming or clinging to the inviolability of nature and of life.

Emboldened by the financial promise of a bestseller, a Guggenheim fellowship, and a bit of prize money, Carson resigned from government service in 1952 and gave herself to her writing. She had already started research for what would be the last of her ocean trilogy, *The Edge of the Sea.* This was to be no mere field guide or catalog for collectors, but an intimate walk along the coastal beaches of the Atlantic shore, looking at and understanding what was there. Carson wanted to make the public aware of the mysterious lives of creatures found among widely diverse habitats and to interpret shore life in terms of its relation to the environment. As narrator, Carson illustrates "the essential unity that binds life to the earth" as she moves from the beaches of Maine to Florida and urges her readers to preserve these unique areas "between the tide lines." *The Edge of the Sea* was graced with some of Carson's most lyrical prose, but its underlying message continued to be cautionary. Like her two previous sea books, individual humans are singularly absent from the scene she describes, but the impact of human activity is everywhere. She asks readers to look more carefully, to take more care of what they find, all the while sharing her own joy in every manifestation of life. *The Edge of the Sea* was published in 1955. It marked the end of her "biography of the sea." Brimming with ideas for other things she wanted to write about, she was obligated first to finish some of the work she had postponed.

In 1953 Carson had agreed to write a book for the distinguished Harper series World Perspectives, edited by Ruth Nanda Anshen, a philosopher known for publishing books on important universal themes. Anshen had asked Carson to write about an aspect of evolution, but by 1956 Carson had decided her next book should be "on the relation of life to its environment." She suggested *Remembrance of Earth* as the title, and then put the book out of mind while she took care of more immediate commitments: a television script on clouds, an article for *Woman's Home Companion* titled "Help Your Child to Wonder," and her private efforts to save a particularly beloved piece of "lost woods" near her cottage in Maine. By the time Carson returned to the project in late 1957, the context of her vision had changed and so had her sense of urgency.

During the same cold war years that she had been roaming the windswept shores of the Atlantic coast, insisting that "neither man nor any other living creature may be studied or comprehended apart from the world in which he lives," the world of science had been revolutionized. The consequent specialization and compartmentalization of science and its remoteness from the average citizen increasingly troubled her. She was unhappy that the facts of science seemed more and more the prerogative of a small number of men, isolated in their laboratories, removed from public dialogue or responsibility. Carson insisted that the "realities of science are the realities of life itself," and she was equally certain that the public had the right to know what was being done in the name of scientific innovation. In letters to friends, Carson mentioned the successful launch of Sputnik I and the disturbing implications she found in this "human eye of intrusion" into a dimension of nature she had previously regarded as sacrosanct.

Carson had also been presented with other irrefutable evidence of how scientific knowledge was being misapplied to the social fabric of life. Friends in her local Audubon Society were alarmed by the U.S. Department of Agriculture's plans to spray thousands of crops and forests with powerful synthetic chemical pesticides — products of wartime science applied with peacetime technology. These new chemicals were the agricultural equivalent of the atomic bomb — and promised to redefine the ancient warfare between farmer and insect. Carson realized that the American public knew as little about the long-term effects of these chemical weapons as they did about the effects of atomic radiation. She understood that the tools of the conquest of nature were not only bombs and weapons but the thoughts, attitudes, and prejudices of the humans who controlled the machines. It was not the atomic bomb, the cold war, or the program to eradicate the fire ant, however, that finally forced her to recognize this new reality. Rather, her perspective was changed by what she understood was happening to the sea and to the life that it carried. She was forced to admit its mutability by pollution and contamination.

In 1957 Carson had accepted a seemingly simple assignment from the editors of *Holiday Magazine* to write a mood portrait about the seashore before the coming of humankind. She struggled inordinately with an essay that should have been an easy postscript to her trilogy. She really wanted to write about how few wild and pristine shores remained in the world, how alarmingly quickly they were disappearing, and how all life was imperiled by careless human activity, by contamination of the environment.

The article "Our Ever-Changing Shore" was published in July 1958. Carson's poetic plea for preserving wilderness areas of seacoast "where the relations of sea and wind and shore — of living things and their physical world — remain as they have been over the long vistas of time in which man did not exist" was juxtaposed with a new censure of "this space-age universe." In this environment there was "the possibility that man's way is not always best." Along with an elegiac description of the process by which dry land emerged from an ancient and primitive ocean, Carson inserted a plea for the preservation of the seacoasts and tangentially warned of a sinister pollution of the seas. Writing the essay forced Carson to confront the range of contamination from the new products of technology, and the thoughtless application of these products on the fabric of life. After launching such an assault, she sensed that there was no safety for any or all. She had moved from a sense of wonder to a sense of dread.

Carson finished the outline for her proposal for the Harper's World Perspectives series in February 1958, clear in her mind the direction she must take. In a letter to her friend Dorothy Freeman, written while listening to a radio report of the disastrous effort to launch the nation's first space satellite from Cape Canaveral, Florida, Carson explained that the theme of her new book would be as she had always thought it would: "Life and the relations of Life to the physical environment." But she confessed that she had been in denial for quite a long time. "Some of the thoughts that came were so unattractive to me that I rejected them completely, for the old ideas die hard, especially when they are emotionally as well as intellectually dear to one. It was pleasant to believe, for example, that much of Nature was forever beyond the tampering reach of man . . . And to suppose that however the physical environment might mold Life, that Life could never assume the power to change drastically — or even destroy — the physical world." But once admitting that humans seemed likely to take on the functions of God without the wisdom of God, Rachel Carson was prepared to do what she could to keep that hubris in check. In one brief letter, Carson outlined the argument of the book that four years later became *Silent Spring*. Her philosophic and scientific intent never changed, but the book's content was elaborated and enlarged as the evidence of contamination and carelessness mounted.

The apogee of Carson's journey into the beauty and seamlessness of nature had been abruptly and brutally intersected by atomic science and by human-dominated applications of science to the natural world. Although she had begun her literary journey without the need for any humans in her canvas, by 1962 human arrogance and human activity dominated. Carson insisted that humans must reassess their commitment to science and technology in light of their relationship to life. She had passed the point of no return, she explained, since "knowing what I do, there would be no future peace for me if I kept silent."

Her personal journey between despair and hope over the next four years is mirrored in the working titles for her new book. *Remembrance of Life*, the first, and in some ways the one she always felt best expressed what was at risk, was soon replaced with *The Control of Nature* — a title favored by her editor as descriptive of the central problem of human arrogance. But Carson insisted her broader concern was with "what life (and especially man) is doing to the environment" and the deeper significance of the evidence she was uncovering of the vast pollution of the environment.

In the spring of 1960, about the same time that Carson discovered she had breast cancer, she also abandoned another title, *Man Against the Earth*, as misleading. "In my flounderings," she wrote her literary agent, whose opinions on such matters she valued, "I keep asking myself what

I would call it if my theme concerned radiation, having some illogical feeling that would be easier." The parallel between chemically caused cancers and radioactive pollution was clear, but she still insisted that "the basic issue is the contamination of the environment." The following year Carson told her editor, "This is a book about man's war against nature and because man is part of nature it is also inevitably a book about man's war against himself." But war and destruction did not triumph either as a book title or as Carson's final estimate about the future of life.

Rachel Carson spent her final months after the publication of *Silent Spring*, in September 1962, working to ensure that the "stream of life," with all its beauty and wonder, might endure. She had made an eloquent plea, as all prophets do, to "turn away" from what she knew was a collision course. As the public, government, and scientific experts debated her conclusions, Carson addressed a small women's college in Claremont, California. In her speech, "Of Man and the Stream of Time," she never mentioned chemical pesticides, DDT, or the misapplications of science. Instead she addressed the larger problems of changing human attitudes toward nature, and she challenged her listeners to do what they could to curb the rapacious human appetite for control. Conquest, be it of insects, space, disease, or nations, was an attitude based on arrogance. With humility and wonder instead, Carson hoped humankind might yet discover itself as part of nature. "We still have not become mature enough to see ourselves as a very tiny part of a vast and incredible universe, a universe that is distinguished above all else by a mysterious and wonderful unity that we flout at our peril."

Carson died of cancer in April 1964. In her own journey she moved from celebration to despair, but ultimately into possibility. In her deepest being she believed that humans were not isolated and alone, but braided inextricably into the fabric of all life. "Man's ways" were not always best, but despair at the outcome of human domination could never be her final assessment — not when there was any hope that humankind could master its appetites and live cooperatively — not when there was within humankind a powerful "remembrance of life." "Once knowing ourselves as a part of the larger whole," it seemed reasonable to Carson to think humankind might be "persuaded to preserve rather than destroy." In the twenty-first century, with evidence of global damage everywhere around us, I am certain Rachel Carson would still insist we dwell in possibility.

CONTRIBUTORS

BIBLIOGRAPHY

Contributors

Peter Matthiessen's nonfiction includes *The Tree Where Man Was Born*, nominated for the National Book Award, and *The Snow Leopard*, which won it. He is the recipient of the Heinz and the Lannan Lifetime Achievement awards, the Gold Medal in Natural History from the Philadelphia Academy of Sciences, the John Burroughs Medal, the Roger Tory Peterson Medal of the Harvard Museum of Natural History, and many others.

His fiction includes *At Play in the Fields of the Lord* (also an NBA nominee), *Far Tortuga*, and the powerful trilogy that began with *Killing Mister Watson*. He is a member of the American Academy of Arts and Sciences and is also a 1991 laureate of the Global Honor Roll of the UN Environmental Programme.

John Elder has taught English and environmental studies at Middlebury College since 1973. His books include *Imagining the Earth: Poetry and the Vision of Nature*, *Following the Brush*, *Reading the Mountains of Home*, *The Frog Run*, and *Pil-*

grimage to Vallombrosa. With the support of a Guggenheim fellowship, he is presently writing about the future of Vermont's forests. His family operates a sugar bush near their home in the village of Bristol.

Al Gore, the former vice president of the United States, is the chairman of Current TV, an independently owned cable and satellite television network for young people based on viewer-created content and citizen journalism. He is the author of the 1992 bestseller *Earth in the Balance: Ecology and the Human Spirit* and the recent bestseller *An Inconvenient Truth.*

John Hay is the author of *The Great Beach* (winner of the John Burroughs Medal), *The Immortal Wilderness, The Run,* and many other books on nature. He is a past president of the Cape Cod Museum of Natural History and a former professor of environmental studies at Dartmouth College. Among his most recent books are *The Bird of Light* and *A Beginner's Faith in Things Unseen.*

Freeman House is the author of *Totem Salmon: Life Lessons from Another Species,* which was judged the best nonfiction book of 1999 by BABRA and was awarded the American Academy of Arts and Letters' Harold Vursell Award for quality of prose. In 2002, he was the recipient of the John Burroughs Medal for best natural history essay. This essay was written with the assistance of a literary fellowship from the Lannan Foundation.

Linda Lear is the author of the prize-winning biography *Rachel Carson: Witness for Nature* and the editor of *Lost Woods: The Discovered Writing of Rachel Carson.* She is a founder of the Lear/Carson archive at Connecticut College. Her most recent book is *Beatrix Potter: A Life in Nature.*

Jim Lynch has won national journalism awards and has written for newspapers throughout the Pacific Northwest and beyond. His debut novel, *The Highest Tide,* won the Pacific

Northwest Booksellers Award in 2006. He now sails, writes, and lives in Olympia, Washington, with his wife and daughter.

Robert Michael Pyle is the author of fourteen books, including *Chasing Monarchs*, *Where Bigfoot Walks*, and *Wintergreen*, which won the John Burroughs Medal. His most recent book, *Sky Time in Gray's River*, was published by Houghton Mifflin in January 2007. A Yale-trained ecologist and a Guggenheim Fellow, he is a full-time writer living in southwestern Washington.

Janisse Ray is a writer, naturalist, and activist. She is the author of the bestseller *Ecology of a Cracker Childhood*, which won the American Book Award, the Southern Book Critics Circle Award, and the Southern Environmental Law Center Award. Anne Raver of the *New York Times* said, "The forests of the Southeast find their Rachel Carson." She is also the author of *Wild Card Quilt* and *Pinhook: Finding Wholeness in a Fragmented Land.*

Sandra Steingraber is a biologist, author, and cancer survivor. Her books include *Living Downstream: An Ecologist Looks at Cancer and the Environment* and *Having Faith: An Ecologist's Journey to Motherhood.* Currently a distinguished visiting scholar at Ithaca College and a contributing editor at *Orion* magazine, she lives in Ithaca, New York, with her husband and two young children.

Terry Tempest Williams's books include *Refuge: An Unnatural History of Family and Place; An Unspoken Hunger; Desert Quartet; Leap;* and *Red: Passion and Patience in the Desert.* She is the recipient of a John Simon Guggenheim fellowship and a Lannan Literary Award in creative nonfiction. Her work has appeared in *Orion*, *The New Yorker*, *The Nation*, the *New York Times*, *Parabola*, and *The Best American Essays.*

Edward O. Wilson, a Harvard professor for nearly five decades, has conducted field research throughout the world and written more than twenty books, including *The Ants*, *The Diversity of Life*, and *On Human Nature*. His awards include two Pulitzer Prizes and the National Medal of Science.

Rachel Carson Bibliography

BOOKS BY RACHEL CARSON

Under the Sea-Wind

Simon and Schuster, New York, 1941
Büchergilde, Gutenberg, Switzerland, 1945
Oxford University Press, New York, 1952
Staples Press, London, 1952
Amiot-Dumont, Paris, 1952
Garden City Books, New York, 1953
Uitgeverij Born, Assen, the Netherlands, 1953
J. H. Schultz Forlag, Copenhagen, 1953
Tidens förlag, Stockholm, 1953
Edizione Casini, Florence, 1954
New American Library, New York, 1955
New Asia Trading Company, Colombo, Ceylon, 1956
Albert Bonniers, Stockholm, 1963
Panther Books, London, 1966
Vuk Karadzic, Belgrade, Yugoslavia, 1966

The Sea Around Us

Oxford University Press, New York, 1951
Staples Press, London, 1952

Tidens förlag, Stockholm, 1952
Editions Stock, Paris, 1952
J. H. Schultz Forlag, Copenhagen, 1952
Editorial Atlante, Mexico City, 1952
H. Aschehoug and Company, Oslo, 1952
Edizione Casini, Rome, 1952
Uitgeverij Born, Assen, the Netherlands, 1952
Bungai Shunju Shinsha, Tokyo, 1952
Biederstein Verlag, Munich, 1952
Biederstein Verlag (Illustrated Edition), Munich, 1953
Tammi, Helsinki, 1953
Mal og Menning, Reykjavík, 1953
Technichka Kniga, Belgrade, Yugoslavia, 1953
Lipa, Koper, Yugoslavia, 1953
New American Library, New York, 1954
Tauchnitz Verlag, Stuttgart, Germany, 1954
Ikaros, Athens, 1954
Shumawa Publishing House, Rangoon, Burma, 1954
Udom Publishing Company, Bangkok, Thailand, 1954
New Asia Trading Company, Colombo, Ceylon, 1955
Penguin Books, London, 1956
N. Tversky and Company, Tel Aviv, 1956
Editora Nacional, São Paulo, 1956
Kuo Publishing Company, Taipei, Taiwan, 1956
Ulyu Moonhwa Sa, Seoul, Korea, 1956
Sahitya, Prevartaka Co-op Society, Madras, India, 1956
Franklin Publications, Lahore, West Pakistan, 1956
Harsha Printing and Publications, Puttur, Madras, India, 1957
Egyptian Ministry of Education, Cairo, 1957
Allied Publishers, New Delhi, India, 1958
Rajpal and Sons, Delhi, India, 1959
Franklin Publications, Tehran, Iran, 1959
Oxford University Press (Revised Edition), New York, 1961
Prisma, Stockholm, 1962
Editions Stock (Abridged for Africa and Indo-China), Paris, 1962
Wydawniczy, Warsaw, 1962
Em. Quirido Utgeverij, Amsterdam, 1963
Hayakawa Shabo, Tokyo, 1964

Current Books, Madras, India, 1965
Higginbothams, Tamil, India, 1966
Gon-Yaung Press, Rangoon, Burma, 1967
Panther Books, London, 1969
J. H. Schultz Forlag, Copenhagen, 1969
Guilio Einaudi Editore, Turin, 1971

The Sea Around Us
Junior Editions

Golden Press, New York, 1958
William Collins & Sons, London, 1959
Folket I Bild, Stockholm, 1959
Casa Editrice Giuseppe Principato, Milan, 1960
Cocorico, Paris, 1961
Forleget Fremad, Copenhagen, 1961
Zuid-Nederlandse, Antwerp, 1963
Editorial Novaro S.A., México D.F., 1966
Otto Maier Verlag, Ravensburg, Germany, 1968

The Edge of the Sea
with illustrations by Robert Hines

Houghton Mifflin Company, Boston, 1955
Staples Press, London, 1956
Amiot-Dumont, Paris, 1956
Biederstein Verlag, Munich, 1957
New American Library, New York, 1959
Cadmus Books, Eau Claire, Wisconsin, 1965
Panther Books, London, 1965
New American Library, New York, 1971

The Rocky Coast
from The Edge of the Sea, *with photographs by Charles Pratt and drawings by Robert Hines*

McCall Publishing Company, New York, 1971

The Sea
(the three sea books in one volume)

McGibbon and Kee, London, 1964
Panther Books, London, 1967
McGibbon and Kee, London, 1968

Silent Spring

Houghton Mifflin Company, Boston, 1962
Hamish Hamilton, Ltd., London, 1963
Penguin Books, London, 1963
Plon, Paris, 1963
Biederstein Verlag, Munich, 1963
Feltrinelli Editore, Milan, 1963
Gyldendalske Boghandel, Copenhagen, 1963
Tidens förlag, Stockholm, 1963
Tiden Norsk Forlag, Norway, 1963
Tammi, Helsinki, 1963
H. J. W. Becht's Uitgeversmaatschappij N. V., Amsterdam, 1963
Fawcett Publications, New York, 1964
Luis de Caralt, Barcelona, 1964
Companhia Melhoramentos, São Paulo, 1964
Shincho Sha, Tokyo, 1964
Bokforidget Prisma, Stockholm, 1965
Almenna Bokafelagid, Reykjavík, 1965
Tiden Norsk Forlag, Norway, 1966
Editorial Portico, Lisbon, 1966
Teva Ubriuth, Petah Tikvah, Israel, 1966
Livre de Poche, Paris, 1967
Tammi [reprint], Helsinki, 1970
Drzavna Zalozba Slovenije, Ljubljana, Yugoslavia, 1971

The Sense of Wonder
with photographs by Charles Pratt and others

Harper and Row, New York, 1965
Harper and Row, New York, 1967

RACHEL CARSON BIBLIOGRAPHY

MAGAZINE ARTICLES BY RACHEL CARSON

"Undersea" in the *Atlantic Monthly*, September 1937

"How About Citizen Papers for the Starling?" in *Nature Magazine*, June–July 1939

"The Bat Knew It First" in *Collier's*, November 18, 1944

"Ocean Wonderland" in *Transatlantic*, April 1945

"The Bat Knew It First" [condensation] in *Reader's Digest*, August 1945

"The Great Red Tide Mystery" in *Field and Stream*, February 1948

"Lost Worlds: The Challenge of the Islands" in *The Wood Thrush*, May–June, 1949

"The Birth of an Island" in the *Yale Review*, September 1950

"Wealth from the Salt Seas" in *Science Digest*, October 1950

"The Shape of Ancient Seas" in *Nature Magazine*, May 1951

"The Sea" in "Profiles," *The New Yorker*, June 2, 9, 16, 1951

"Why Our Winters Are Getting Warmer" [excerpt from *The Sea Around Us*] in *Popular Science*, November 1951

"The Edge of the Sea" [excerpt from *Under the Sea-Wind*] in *Life*, April 14, 1952

The Edge of the Sea [excerpt] in "Profiles," *The New Yorker*, August 20 and 27, 1955

"The Mystery of Life at the Seashore" [condensation of *The Edge of the Sea*] in *Reader's Digest*, February 1956

"Help Your Child to Wonder" in *Woman's Home Companion*, July 1956

"Help Your Child to Wonder" [condensation] in *Reader's Digest*, September 1956

"Our Ever-Changing Shore" in *Holiday*, July 1958

Silent Spring [excerpts] in "Reporter at Large," *The New Yorker*, June 16, 23, 30, 1962

"Poisoned Waters Kill Our Fish and Wildlife" [excerpt from *Silent Spring*] in *Audubon Magazine*, September 1962

"Beyond the Dreams of the Borgias" [excerpt from *Silent Spring*] in *National Parks Magazine*, October 1962

"Beetle Scare, Spray Planes and Dead Wildlife" [excerpt from *Silent Spring*] in *Audubon Magazine*, November 1962

"Moving Tides" [excerpt from *The Sea Around Us*] in *Motor Boating*, July 1963
"Rachel Carson Answers Her Critics" in *Audubon Magazine*, September 1963
"Miss Carson Goes to Congress" in *American Forests*, October 1963